The Fire Within

Sermons from the Edge of Exile

Dr Allan Boesak

WILD GOOSE PUBLICATIONS
THE IONA COMMUNITY

Copyright © Allan A. Boesak 2004

UK edition first published 2007 by
Wild Goose Publications
4th Floor, Savoy House, 140 Sauchiehall Street, Glasgow G2 3DH, UK
www.ionabooks.com
Wild Goose Publications is the publishing division of the Iona Community.
Scottish Charity No. SCO03794. Limited Company Reg. No. SCO96243.

ISBN 978-1-905010-38-7

First published 2004 by
New World Foundation (incorporating The Institute for Theology and Public Life)
PO Box 2907947, Steenberg, Cape Town, South Africa

Design and setting by DTP Impressions
Cover design by DTP Impressions

We gratefully acknowledge the support of the Drummond Trust,
3 Pitt Terrace, Stirling, in the publication of this book

A catalogue record for this book is available from the British Library.

Overseas distribution:
Australia: Willow Connection Pty Ltd, Unit 4A, 3–9 Kenneth Road, Manly Vale, NSW 2093
New Zealand: Pleroma, Higginson Street, Otane 4170, Central Hawkes Bay
Canada: Novalis/Bayard Publishing & Distribution, 10 Lower Spadina Ave., Suite 400,
Toronto, Ontario M5V 2Z2

Printed by Thomson Litho, East Kilbride, Glasgow

Dedication

In memoriam:
Edward Martin Huenemann:
true theologian, matchless
friend; and that rarest of
beings, a gentle Calvinist.

To Pastor Graham Taff and
the Full Gospel Church in
Paarl who surrounded us
with love and understanding.
You have done more than
you will ever know to let me
taste the grace of God.

In deep gratitude.

CONTENTS

If I say, 'I will not mention Him,
or speak any more in His name,'
then within me there is
something like a burning fire
shut up in my bones;
I am weary with holding it in,
and I cannot.

(Jeremiah 20:9)

Foreword

After a long drought, Allan Boesak has come up with a new book of his sermons. Its release indicates that he has not been paralysed by what may have been traumatic experiences in his recent past and which may have made him feel at the 'edge of exile'. On the contrary, the title suggests that he was burning to say what he felt should be said. And he continued to do that when opportunities presented themselves and from the platform that he knows best, namely the pulpit. Through this publication, the contents of his sermons become available to a broader audience.

Allan Boesak has not been, and will not be, silenced by the circumstances that surround him. It could not be done during the years of political oppression and it has not happened even during the first ten years of democracy and the controversies that surrounded his person in recent times. In the past he was dauntless in his exposition of the Word to the injustice of apartheid. In these sermons he identifies and makes the Word speak to the issues of injustices that seem to have remained unattended and sometimes have, perhaps conveniently, not been brought to the table of transformation. It includes the present manifestations of racism, of the widening discrepancy between the rich and the poor, HIV/Aids, homosexuality, etc. In dealing with the status quo regarding these issues, he does not only challenge our national inequities, but also the global threats of war, and the environment, and the graceless powers responsible for them.

We all know Allan Boesak is a very gifted person. His sharp intellect, his literary and communicative skills, his scholarly groundedness, his self-confidence, are all excellently exhibited in these sermons. Added to this is the fact that he makes it clear that he speaks from a Christian perspective of a Calvinist brand and with an ecumenical disposition.

These sermons have meaning for all of us. To students, they teach us how to interface the context of the Biblical text with the contemporary context in order to give meaning to our existence now. To pastors and preachers, they illustrate how to dialogue with the text in order to extract from it the fullest potential and wealth of meaning contained in it. To the ordinary reader, they confirm that the gospel message remains a message of hope and inspiration, irrespective of how depressing one's personal situation may be or how incomplete we may experience society. Whoever reads them cannot but be spiritually enriched and motivated.

G D Cloete
Professor Emeritus
New Testament Studies
University of the Western Cape

Preface

The hard part wasn't writing down these sermons from my preaching notes and preparing them for publication. The hard part was getting into the pulpit and preaching them. Sometimes, it is the other way around, as has been observed. One preaches in a loving, responsive community of faith, where one knows one's listeners and they know you. The context of the sermon is known and understood. When those sermons are published, the intimacy is lost, the context is hard to communicate and can certainly not be recreated. One has to explain things that were immediate and understandable to the congregation where the sermon was first preached.

This time, for me, it was the preaching that was difficult. This might sound strange coming from someone who has been preaching for more than thirty years, and whose sermons have been published before. Those sermons, however, preached and published during the times of our struggle against apartheid, were sermons in which I was called to be the voice of the voiceless, crying out for justice for the sake of the people. The sermons in this book were not specifically prepared and delivered within the context of the struggle (although even now I cannot escape from the hard truth that the struggle is not over, simply different), but much more in the context of my own personal struggle, my own pain, confronting my own deepest fears. The reader will find some of these sermons intensely personal, framed within the perplexity of my own voicelessness: how can the one made voiceless be speaking the Word of God to others?

So let me explain. In 1994, I was accused of theft and fraud. Only a few months after South Africa's liberation, my own life, and that of my family, was uprooted and thrown into the middle of a storm such as we had never before known. I spent a year in prison. In the eyes of many, I have become a 'one time preacher/theologian/politician', virtually written off as a fraud and a betrayer of the cause I had given my life to. As such, I had nothing worthwhile, or truthful, to say.

When, in the last two years or so before the trial, churches in the United States, and later churches in South Africa, invited me to preach, I found it first hard to believe, and then to accept. I was beset with doubt. How could I preach again? What did these people have in mind? I had been told enough times that I would remain 'untouchable' until I was cleared by some court. Was this a set-up then? And now that that court has spoken, what is it that they really wanted? Deep down, I knew I had to face something else: I was afraid.

I was afraid of peoples' reactions. Most of them, I thought, would think, how can he, *how dare he* preach to us? I know that God's own justice will one day be my vindication, but how thin that sounds as the years go by! And how does one explain the ruthless subtleties of South African politics that have brought me to this point? Besides, as Jesus said, 'prophets are not honoured in their own land'. In our age's global communication revolution what Jesus saw as 'own land' is now the world. With CNN, BBC World News and the Internet, that prophet has nowhere to go, and in disgrace a 'prophet' is a world-wide joke. But our God is a God of wonders. I have been returned to a warm, loving, supporting community of faith. Love has removed the fear. The healing has begun, and the nurturing is part of God's wondrous restoration.

I was afraid of the press. The religious press included. What would they do with a story about my preaching again? Even in less controversial circumstances, I have seen them twist my sermons to suit their own political agenda and sometimes they have reacted with a viciousness and fury that invite serious analysis. When, on the day I was released from prison, I preached on Psalm 126, taken up in this book, yet another media guardian of democracy spoke of me as 'the demagogue of the poor' who needed to be 'disciplined' by the African National Congress (ANC). This is the English-language, liberal, so-called anti-apartheid press I am quoting, mind you. In reading these sermons, the reader must judge for themselves.

I was afraid of the political dynamics in South Africa. The ANC is the people's government. It is *our* liberation movement. There are many good reasons why those of us who come out of the struggle do not want to be misused by the political opposition, which we inevitably are when we raise points of criticism vis-à-vis our politics. That has made many of us reticent to speak prophetically to our society. We do not want to be used by the ANC's political opponents, who also happen to be *our* political opponents. Their criticism of the ANC government is strident, trivial, and in our view, galling in its glaring hypocrisy. *Our* motivations might be honest, but *theirs* certainly are not and we hate to be placed in a position like that. This goes a long way in explaining the strange quiet of some of the anti-apartheid churches in South Africa today.

But, there is something else. There are those in the African National Congress who have sometimes shown themselves to not welcome criticism readily, however well-meant, even from within. On occasion some in the leadership have been harsh with black journalists, intellectuals and clerics who have criticised the government, and many ANC supporters embrace this ethos, branding any critical question raised as 'disloyalty'. I have myself felt the pressure after my open letter from prison to an ANC minister in the previous cabinet. It is not a comfortable position to be in. Moreover, the political process in South Africa, more specifically the negotiated settlement, the government's economic policies and the 'truth and reconciliation' process are strangely, but understandably seen by the white establishment, and by the privileged new elite to whom they are greatly beneficial, as sacred. To criticise these processes is regarded as almost blasphemous. It is not for nothing that it is precisely that fiery prophet, Amos, who in his turbulent day finds reason to caution 'the prudent' to 'keep silent in such a time; for it is an evil time' (Amos 5:13). Most preachers are doing just that. They shut up. But there is a whole generation of preachers who have had to stand up against the dreaded apartheid regime and its minions in the media and the western world, and who have found strength and courage in the gospel of Jesus Christ. For them, speaking prophetically to our new government and to our people in this country is not a sign of enmity but of love, not of alienation from our democratic ideal but of commitment to it. They are speaking in the hope that our new government will know this and listen. But should the government refuse both to know and to listen, we will have to speak anyway. Loyalty to our Lord Jesus Christ remains higher than loyalty to any political party.

It goes deeper still. Throughout this painful period I have been struggling with my pain, my anger with God and with the incomprehensibility of my own situation. I struggled to understand what God has in mind, what God's promises are worth. It seemed that every morning I overcame my confusion and fear, only to be overwhelmed by my doubt as night fell. In the morning I praise God for God's faithfulness; at night I curse the day I was born. In the morning I am convinced of the power of God; at night I am bewildered by the power of evil. My faith drives me to my knees; my unbelief drives me up the wall. For one caught up in the vortex of such contradictions it is not easy to preach. It is only the faithfulness of God that has brought me back from the brink of this devastation.

Still, I feel less like Amos, 'The lion has roared; who will not fear? The LORD has spoken; who can but prophesy?' (Amos 3:8); and much more like Jeremiah, 'O LORD, you have seduced me, and I was seduced … For the Word of the LORD has become for me a reproach and derision all day long.' (Jeremiah 20:7, 8) Like Jeremiah, tossed between praising and cursing, between belief and unbelief, I too would sometimes rather do anything else but preach God's Word. I think I am too vulnerable, too wounded already, and sometimes I wonder whether those scars will ever heal.

But like Jeremiah, I have been overpowered, and God has prevailed. Against my better judgement, I have preached. Like Jeremiah, I have discovered that inescapable truth that every person called of God must face, and deal with, namely that such a one cannot escape the power of God. Resistance is futile, for, in the words of that marvelous prophet which serve as leitmotif of this book,

> … within me there is
> something like a burning fire
> shut up in my bones;
> I am weary of holding it in.
> and I cannot. (Jeremiah 20:9)

So in the end, the question was not so much, 'Shall I dare to preach', but rather, 'How dare I not preach?' Not so much, 'What if the media misuse this?', or 'What if some comrades are upset?', but rather, 'What if I disobey God?' The fire, like the one Moses saw, cannot be quenched, and I have given up trying to fight God. Hence the sub-title of this collection, 'Sermons from the Edge of Exile'. The years between 1995 and 2001 were like exile; from my country and from the church. But when the doors of the church closed for me in South Africa, it was the church in the United States that opened its doors for me. It was an act of love and acceptance that recalled me, restored me, redeemed me. It was an act that celebrated the love of Christ and in so doing fulfilled the law of Christ (Galatians 6:2). So the 'exile' was not total. I was caught at the edge of it, and turned away from it. There is a great joy in this discovery, and I hope that joy is as apparent in the reading of these sermons as it was in my preaching them.

I am speaking especially of Lafayette/Orinda Presbyterian Church, California USA, Allen Temple Baptist Church, Oakland, California under the inspiring leadership of Dr J Alfred Smith Snr, and the American Baptist Seminary of the West at Berkeley, California under President Keith Russell. I am speaking also of all the churches in this country, too numerous to mention, that have since become a spiritual home, and of the many Christian leaders who have embraced me with so much love and compassion. My humble words of thanks will always be inadequate, but God knows my heart. With Ephesians 3,

> I pray that, according to the riches of his glory, God may
> grant that you may be strengthened in your inner being
> with power through his Spirit, and that Christ may dwell
> in your hearts through faith, as you are being rooted
> and grounded in love. I pray that you may have the
> power to comprehend, with all the saints, what is the
> breadth and length and height and depth, and to know
> the love of Christ that surpasses knowledge, so that you
> may be filled with all the fullness of God.

As I said, the preaching that made this collection possible was not easy to do. It would have been immeasurably harder without the constant help of my wife, Elna who, as always in the last thirteen years, has been an inspiration, an exciting intellectual sparring partner, and a healing reminder of the presence of God in our lives despite everything. I am also grateful to Rev Jan de Waal and the Institute for Theology and Public Life and its partner in the Netherlands, the Netherlands Protestant Church, under whose auspices several seminars on preaching have been held. Those persons who attended these workshops will recognise some of these sermons. I thank them for their critical participation and support, as I thank the Institute for its willingness to publish these sermons as part of their programme, making them accessible to a wider audience. My prayer is that in their published form, these sermons will serve as inspiration to many, and strengthen their commitment to live the gospel of salvation in the new and challenging times in which we live and work. May they also be of help to those preachers of the gospel who, through the pressures of our changed and constantly changing situations and the terrible loneliness that the ministry sometimes brings, feel themselves exiled, pushed to the edge of their existence, feeling they are living their calling in the margins of both church and society. They are not alone and that situation is never the last word.

This book is dedicated to the memory of Edward Huenemann, long time theologian of the Presbyterian Church in the USA. Our friendship lasted for more than twenty years until his death in 1996. I count myself very fortunate indeed to have benefited from his immense knowledge and his vivid theological mind. Seldom have I known a friend so loyal and a theologian so thoughtful. His death left the church the poorer, but his legacy will forever enrich our lives. It is also dedicated in humble gratitude to Graham Taff, pastor and loyal friend, truly God's hand of comfort in some of the most difficult times of my life. To God be the glory.

Allan Boesak

The Second Week After Easter, 2004

The Tale of the Tower of Fear

Now the whole world had one language and the same words. And as they migrated from the east, they came upon a plain in the land of Shinar and settled there. And they said to one another, 'Come, let us make bricks, and burn them thoroughly.' And they had brick for stone, and bitumen for mortar. Then they said, 'Come, let us build ourselves a city, and a tower, with its top in the heavens, and let us make a name for ourselves; otherwise we shall be scattered abroad upon the face of the earth.' The LORD came down to see the city and the tower, which mortals had built. And the LORD said, 'Look, they are one people, and they all have one language; and this is only the beginning of what they will do; nothing that they will propose to do will now be impossible for them. Come, let us go down, and confuse their language there, so that they will not understand one another's speech.' So the LORD scattered them abroad from there over the face of all the earth, and they left building the city. Therefore it was called Babel, because there the LORD confused the language of all the earth; and from there the LORD scattered them abroad over the face of all the earth.

Genesis 11:1-9

1

This is a story fraught with difficulties and it comes with a whole history of misunderstandings. I will not say that the story of Babel in that sense is 'worse' than other biblical stories. But it did inspire some unique interpretations.

For some, Genesis 11 is the explanation for the origin of languages. It is, I think *they* think, the perfect beginner's tool for Esperanto. For others, Babel is the personification of the evils of urbanisation and modernisation versus rural simplicity and spirituality. Here is the beginning of all our modern ailments: we leave the land where we were close to the earth and our own origins, and move to the sprawling cities, the breeding place of vice and sin. Our relationship with the land is lost, as is our relationship with our neighbours. A relationship of mutual concern and care is replaced by alienation, distrust and enmity. It ends as it had to: with total confusion, misunderstanding, dispersion.

Still others see Babel as biblical imagery of the growth of the world's financial empires. The tower of Babel equals the towers of the financial houses on Wall Street: symbols of ruthless manipulation of money markets and of the concomitant helplessness of the powerless masses who do not begin to understand the intricacies of the financial wizardry that shapes their world and controls their fate. At the same time Babel is read as a foreshadow of humankind's technological progress, reaching frightening heights, eventually overreaching ourselves, inviting God's wrath and punishment. Advances in medical science, genetic manipulation and human cloning – possibilities and now realities that make doctors and scientists into gods – Babel is the mother of it all.

Close to this view is the understanding of the sin of the people of Babel as human pride, which always leads to arrogance and hubris. The seeds of doom lie in the boastful 'Come let us build ourselves a city, and a tower with its top in the heavens, and let us make a name for ourselves …'. There is the mindless ambition of the builders of Babel. The action of God resulting in the confusion of language is God's way of putting them in their place. In this sense, Babel becomes more than story: it is prophecy, and its final fulfilment, keeping in mind the state of the world, cannot be far off.

In the literature of the far religious right, the story of Babel foretells the sinful effort of human beings to 'be of one accord'. Efforts toward what they call 'world government' as reflected in institutions like the United Nations and other international institutions are modern towers of Babel seeking to destroy the individuality of nations and persons, trying to place 'God-fearing' nations under the heel of the godless. Usually, for this group, the World Council of Churches would fall into this category as well. I do not believe that the story of the tower of Babel wants to tell us any of this.

However, by far the most imaginative misreading of the story of the tower, I think, can be found in the theology of the white Afrikaans Reformed churches in their moral and theological justification and defence of apartheid. Locating the sin of Babel in verse 1, apartheid theology interpreted it as a deliberate attempt to defy God's command given at creation (Genesis 1:28), and repeated to Noah (Genesis 9:1, 7), that humankind should divide into separate peoples with different cultures, each on their own. Because this division is the indispensable basis for the peoples of the world to spread out and *be apart*, in other words, to 'fill the earth' in obedience to God's command, the very idea of 'one city, one people, one language' is a defiance of God.

The unity of Babel as described in Genesis 11:1 and 6 is in itself offensive and contrary to God's creational order, proof of the sinfulness, disobedience and arrogance of humankind. God's act of confusing the language is therefore much more than just a question of language. It is also an assertion of God's original command that humankind should split up into different, distinct peoples with different languages and cultures, living within predetermined parameters of their separate places. It is a deliberate act of *segregation* and apartheid, nullifying Babel's bent towards integration.

Since the action of the Reformed churches of the world to declare apartheid a sin and its theological justification a heresy, and especially since the end of apartheid as official government policy in South Africa, this theology has lost its power. Among representatives of these churches one would today find few who would still defend this discredited viewpoint. This is not to say, however, that it has lost its relevance for those who still believe that the separation of the races can be justified from Scripture, if not in society, then at least in their churches.

II

All these readings are interesting, sometimes curious, but they do not pinpoint what I believe to be the sin of Babel as depicted in our story. That sin lies, I think, in verse 4:

> Come, let us build ourselves a city, and a tower with
> its top in the heavens, and let us make a name for
> ourselves; otherwise we shall be scattered abroad upon
> the face of the earth.

It is these words, and especially the last part of the verse, that give away the game. And it is here, not in verse 1, where the act of disobedience and defiance lies. For the tale of Babel is indeed told to show the contrast between God's purposes and the ideas of sinful, prideful humankind. And sure, the narrator raises amused chuckles from his listeners as he describes the building process in detail; as Babel reaches high to make for themselves a 'name' with their tower with its 'top in the heavens'. Every faithful Jew knows the futility and preposterousness of such endeavours. But by the time we get to verse 6, when Yahweh has to 'come down' to see this city and its heaven-high tower, our story has them rolling in the aisles. It is, after all, only a city and a tower 'which mortals had built'. No matter how high they go; God still has to 'come down'.

But underneath all the amusement, Israel knew this was serious business. The story of Babel's tower contradicts everything that has been God's intention. This is a story of humankind in revolt against

God and all creation, of a people at cross-purposes with God, in denial of their own destiny and their very reason for being. Israel knows: the tale is about a city and a tower, but what is at stake is the future of the world. Israel knows: what we see here is not just the silly plans of foolish human beings, but an attack upon the purposes of God.

The contrast with these purposes of God, the contrast between the acts of God and the acts of the people of Babel cannot be denied. God said, 'Let us make humankind …'. *They* said, 'Let us make bricks …'. God said, '… in our image and our likeness …'; *they* said, 'Let us make a name for ourselves …'. God blessed them and said, 'Be fruitful and multiply, and fill the earth, and subdue it, and have dominion …'; *they* said, 'let us build a city, and a tower with its top in the heavens … otherwise we shall be scattered abroad upon the face of the earth'.

The images emerging out of this contrast are completely different; they are, in fact, opposing. God creates humankind in order to go out, fill the earth, work it, subdue it, shape it until it becomes space for life, a dwelling place for God and all God's creation. In order to do this, God does not command or compel them, but instead 'blessed them and said'. This has at least two implications. To work the earth, to 'have dominion', is not a curse or an order, it is a blessing. Secondly, this means that humankind is to be a blessing to the rest of creation. It was always thus. God blesses Abraham not just for his own sake, but to be a blessing to the nations. In the same way, God blesses Joseph not to wield power for power's sake, but to save a whole people. By linking 'dominion' to 'blessing' the whole idea of 'lording it over' with its overtones of violence is subverted and effectively set aside. It is a blessing meant to serve.

But that means that human beings are called to become engaged in this world, in the affairs of history. To 'subdue the earth' must not be understood in simple agrarian terms. It has social, political, economic implications. God's wish is for human beings to build, to plant, to sow, to harvest, to create a world in which all this is possible. To make right what is wrong. And to do that *together with others*.

It means also, almost as an inevitable consequence, opening oneself to others, their love and compassion, but also their critique and correction. 'Subduing the earth' is both a human and humanising effort, an activity which calls for community and togetherness and agitates against separation, isolationism and the inwardness of self-preservation. It implies, too, an understanding of our creaturely relatedness, of our oneness with the rest of creation, and opens us up to the blessing and critique of the earth and the heavens.

But to do this, to be a part of all this, which is God's purpose, means that we must be ready to be 'scattered'. We cannot do any of this while sitting fearfully in our own little corner, fiercely guarding our own little piece of turf. To be scattered means to be willing to lose a bit of ourselves, of our own identity, in order to gain the greater purpose of our humanness. And this is what the Babelonians feared most. Building a city, building a tower, making a name for themselves – all of this is necessary, but purely preliminary to the real thing: to prevent being scattered. The Babelonians found being in the world, doing God's will, serving creation and humankind, getting their hands dirty in the affairs of being human, unthinkable. That vulnerability of community, that woundability of openness, scares the Babelonians to death. So Babel closes up.

It is not as if the Babelonians are doing this out of ignorance. No, they know exactly what the score is. There are no surprises here. They understand only too well what the LORD requires. Hence their vehement resistance. No less than three times we hear the words the people of Babel fear most, the words that form the heart of the matter: 'Otherwise we shall be scattered ...'.

And not just scattered, but scattered 'abroad upon the face of the earth' (v.4). And indeed, that is precisely the LORD's intention. There are no half measures. Then the narrator repeats twice the fact that God's purposes shall not be thwarted. Babel is called to order by the disorder of the confusion, and the LORD 'scattered' them 'over the face of all the earth'. (vv. 8, 9) That is what God wants, and that is what Babel refuses to do. And that is the sin of Babel.

Babel places a towering correction on all that God intends. That tower is a heaven-high 'NO!' to God. Babel chooses to remain in one place, safeguarded by walls of brick and tar. The Babelonians do not want to risk losing themselves in the world – there is too much to lose. It is not just that they experience angst as in their 'finitude, frailty and individual mortality', they face the vastness of the world, as one commentator explains. It is that their unity, their being together, their sameness, have become so precious that they did not dare risk it in confrontation with the world. What drove them was not the preservation of the world, but preservation of *self*. What motivated them was not to share God's blessing with creation, but to keep the blessing for themselves. What they had in mind was not the salvation of the world, but the self-satisfied glorification of Babel.

Besides, they knew: once you do that, once you open yourself up to the world and become engaged in the affairs of the world, you risk breaking the unity. You invite dissension. If you point out the wrongs *outside*, pretty soon someone will point put the wrongs on the *inside*. And before you know it you will have to make choices, and that brings tensions.

So let us prevent that, they tell themselves. Let us build a city, with walls to keep the world out, so that we do not have to see the world, its pain, the suffering of its people, their needs or the challenges they pose. 'Let us make a name for ourselves.' Let us become the envy of those who are foolish enough to respond to God's will. Let us show our technological prowess to the world and let them see the great heights a people united can attain. This is the epitome of Babel's civilization: life without God, greatness without risk, security without humanity. Let us revel in our isolation. Let us then celebrate our achievement: one people, one language, one goal. One city where we all think alike and speak alike. 'Oh blessed uniformity!' is the battle hymn of the Republic of Babel.

Let us build a tower, they say. They mean a *ziggurat*, a temple tower, a steeple with steps, something like a human-made holy mountain. It is a sign of communication with heaven. The steps are not for the people to go up to heaven, but for the gods to come down to speak with their supplicants. But that high tower 'with its top in the heavens' signifies more than just their religiosity. It is simultaneously a witness to their power, high enough for all to see. And it is entirely fitting that the power is expressed in their affinity to, nay more, their *familiarity* with their gods. So the tower symbolises their power and their religion, their achievements as well as their life style, their theology that fits the ideology of unity, power, self-preservation and self-sufficiency. The tower, in all its intimidating strength and glory, says it all: Babel has made it. It needs no one. It has communication with the gods of its choosing while it cuts itself off from the world. For them, that is enough. For them, that is the glory of their self-centered existence, the essence of their carefully contained faith.

III

And so the tale of the tower of Babel, that tower that was supposed to represent power and high achievement, independence and self-sufficiency, turns out to be a tale of a tower of fear. Fear of love and openness, of engagement and humanness, fear of life itself. But it certainly was not fear of the LORD. It also turns out to be a devastating critique of the kind of theology that seeks to sanctify apartheid, separateness and racism. It is a critique also of all theology that is no more than a religion of the dominant culture, revelling in its rituals of self-endorsement, while drowning out the dissident voices that speak a language other than the dominant, and accepted one.

It is a critique of all theology which becomes the religiosity of the powerful, leaving the powerless and the poor, the weak and the needy to languish outside in the shadow of the tower. It is a revolt against all theology that pictures God as waving the flag of unrepentant nationalism, making God the author of selfish self-preservation and the source of self-sufficient pietism while they keep the suffering of the world outside their gates. Their unity is patently false because it is the unity of coercion. Their sameness is in suppression of dissent; their 'name' is the notoriety of self-deception; their greatness is in denial of love; their language is the language of self-congratulatory pride.

'And the LORD said, look, they are one people, and they have all one language; and this is only the beginning of what they will do; nothing that they propose will now be impossible for them.' (v.6) These are strange, ominous sounding words. It is not, as some have suggested, that God is 'threatened' by an autonomous, free-thinking human being, wanting always to keep us 'small' in order to keep us forever dependent on the divine power. The power God himself had invested in human beings at creation remains irreversible, and God is not regretting that. God is worrying about something else.

What was intended as a blessing for humankind, has now been turned into a threat to humankind. The unity of humanity has been turned into a dangerous sameness. The fantasy of our creativity, which blossoms in our obedience to God, has been harnessed, compressed into a slave mentality that has lost all sense of freedom. No one dares to break the pattern of speech. Raising doubts about the ways of the people is a threat to the unity of the people. Raising questions about the walls around the city is an onslaught on the security of the city. Questioning the tower is a sin against the gods.

But the strangeness of God's words does not end there. 'This is only the beginning,' God says, 'nothing that they propose will now be impossible for them'. God sounds scared, and rightly so. But the LORD is not afraid for Himself, He is afraid for us. When there is just sameness, when all must speak the same language, when dissident voices are silenced, and when those who turn against the tower are crushed by the tower, then indeed nothing that they propose to do will be impossible, for there is no way to stop them. And this is only the beginning! Who knows to what terrible depths humanity will be plunged by those drunk with the power of the tower.

How right the Bible is. For have we not seen this again and again, throughout our history? How quickly did the voice of Hitler become the voice of all Germany, relegating all critical voices to the sidelines, or to the prison cells, finally silencing them before the firing squad, or like Dietrich Bonhoeffer, on the gallows? And how easy it became for almost everyone to be deaf to the voices of those in the extermination camps, outside the walls and under that Aryan tower? And how important, how necessary, how indispensable it is for dictators to emphasise the 'unity' of the people, since it is this bogus unity that guarantees their position of power. They absolutely cannot live without the cry, 'One Leader, one People, one Country, one Flag!' And they spell them with capitals too.

How rapidly has the 'anti-communist' cry of Eugene McCarthy become the righteous voice of outraged, paranoid America, devouring common sense, reason and civility, substituting the God of the Bible for the god of mercenary political expediency? And how quickly have so many in the Christian church joined the thunderous voice of self-righteous politics, enhanced a thousand-fold by the media, hungry for sensation and brooking no dissent, sanctioning the inauguration of President Bush's 'new world order', and blessing the war on Iraq, because it was 'God's war'? How hard it was then, for honourable men and women to be heard? How were the prophets ridiculed, who knew, and saw, what this hysteria would leave in its wake? Those who were not part of the sameness, who did not bow down at Babel's altars, or sang in Babel's choir, were cast out the gates, marginalised by the powers of the tower. And it does not end there. When, in the light of the hundreds of thousands of Iraqi children dying from starvation and lack of medical care because of American policies, Secretary of State Madeline Albright was asked whether the policies were worth the price, she answered without even blinking, 'It is worth it.' God was right: 'Nothing that they propose to do will be impossible for them ...'.

Because the voices of dissent and prophecy have virtually been silenced, the United States, under the guise of the new 'Patriot Laws' has fortified that tower. The unilaterally declared war on Iraq in 2003 has turned into an unmitigated disaster, the language of unbridled militancy and righteous triumphalism is now drowned in the cries of pain and deeds of shame that seem to go on and on. Those weapons of mass destruction were never found, and the innocent thousands who have died cannot be resurrected. It is frightening, but true: 'Nothing that they propose will be impossible for them …'.

It is supreme irony that the new South Africa has taken over from the old that which was so hallowed in white, apartheid South Africa. Like the monuments of the heroes and the remnants of the policies of white South Africa, the tower of Babel still towers over the lives of our people. The official ideology says, 'We are a miracle', 'Apartheid is dead', 'Racism no longer exists', 'We are the rainbow nation'. That is the defensive, albeit futile mantra in the media. Those who disagree, who point to the rampant racism, both inherited from the past and revived by the present; who try to tell South Africa that we are still two nations, with a growing chasm between the poor and the rich, including the new elite, are 'enemies of democracy', 'clinging to outdated sentiments'. The dissident voices who defend the poor are called 'demagogues of the poor'.

The media, the politicians, the outside world are impressed by the 'process of national reconciliation' because their interests are served by it. Everyone must agree. Those who differ, who for the sake of true reconciliation ask questions about the genuineness of the process, who question the sincerity of security policemen and torturers who 'declare' their version of the truth and walk out smiling, are condemned. Those who wonder at a process where the evildoers are not required to repent, and where whole sections of the apartheid apparatus, like the judiciary, are left untouched for political reasons, leaving one of the central pillars of the apartheid state unrepentant and untransformed, are branded renegades. Those who have problems with a theological curiosity where a government-appointed body has been sanctioned to 'reconcile' vicariously on behalf of the nation, who raise questions about the biblical validity of it all, are attacked, accused of having an 'unforgiving spirit', not being 'Christian' and disloyal.

And it is only the beginning! Indeed, nothing that they propose will now be impossible for them.

So now God acts. 'Come, let us go down, and confuse their language there …' (v.7). 'Just as God deprives Adam and Eve of the paradise where God had originally set them, God now deprives humankind of the unity and mutual understanding which God gave them but which they have now misused,' writes one commentator. That might be true. But I would like to suggest something else.

God is not depriving humankind of anything. We have short-changed ourselves! 'Confusing their language' here means breaking that sinful uniformity; breaking the silence, breaking down the monopoly of sameness, breaking down the hegemony of the tower. Breaking the monopoly, confusing the language of subservient sameness means creating room for dissent, making space for criticism, opening a breach in the walls of this enclosed city, subverting the foundations of the tower. It means letting in the light of prophecy.

God knows when it is needed.

- Michaia ben Imla, facing the prophets of the court who could only pronounce the wishes of the king. 'As the LORD lives, whatever the LORD says to me, that I will speak' (1 Kings 22:14).
- Elijah, facing King Ahab, knowing that 400 prophets of Baal spoke only what the king wanted to hear. 'I have not troubled Israel, but you have, and your father's house, because you have forsaken the commandments of the LORD and followed the Baals' (1 Kings 18:18).
- Dietrich Bonhoeffer, in Hitler's Germany, 'Whoever cannot cry for Jews, cannot sing Gregorian hymns.'
- Martin Luther King, in an era amazingly adapted to violence, 'We must be like Jesus of Nazareth, who had the courage to say, "he who lives by the sword shall perish by the sword".'
- Rosa Parks, whose silent protest by remaining in her seat in a segregated bus spoke louder than and outlasted all the harsh voices of segregation and hatred. And started a movement that forever changed America and the world.

One of the quiet, unsung heroes of the church in South Africa is a man called Herbert Brand. Brought up in the white Dutch

Reformed Church, under the influence of the church leadership led by men like Dr Koot Vorster, brother of the Prime Minister in the 1960s and early 1970s, Brand became a formidable spokesperson for apartheid. Then God changed his mind and his life and Rev Herbert Brand became a lone voice in the white church. At every synod meeting he rose, and with his trembling voice, hampered by a speech impediment, he witnessed to the truth of the gospel, and to his conviction that the white church will never be a true church unless it confesses apartheid as a sin and declares its own defence of it heresy. Every year he spoke, every year he was subjected to jibes and was the butt of jokes and snide remarks. It was excruciatingly painful to watch, but at the same time the courage of this quiet man made him sound like Chrysostom. Much has changed in the white Dutch Reformed church. The Confession of Belhar has been accepted by many, the movement toward unity has been given new impetus and some churches are already working together as one, despite the hesitation of synods. Inasmuch as this change is taking place, I believe much of it is owed to the courageous testimony of this quiet man. Herbert Brand's life stands as a flaming testimony to resistance to the tower and his persistent, subversive piety will yet prove to be his church's salvation.

All these voices spoke in a different language, refusing to bow to the oppressing, albeit comfortable sameness of their age. They dared to challenge the uniformity of Babel, dared to point out the cracks in the wall, pleaded for the breaking down of the wall, dared to show up the shaky foundations of that staggering tower. And they were, God be praised, not the only ones. The list goes on.

IV

So the curious thing is that the confusion of languages in Babel teaches us that we must learn to speak. Not the language of comfortable uniformity, but the language of prophecy and courage and daring and truth. We are called to speak out against the return of race as the determining factor in relationships and in South African society. Against the inwardness that is the justification of fear: the fear of the other, fear of the stranger, of the one who is different (for example, gays and lesbians); fear of the world. The fear to lose ourselves, to give ourselves, to open ourselves for the sake of the other. The fear which was the fear of Babel, of which that tower was such a frightening symbol.

But: is this utter confusion the final word? Does the story end there? Let's take a look. What follows in Genesis 11 is fairly innocuous, and frankly, slightly boring. Suddenly this gripping tale of the city with its tower tapers off into this bland repetition of names: Shem, Arpachshad, Shelah and Eber. Peleg, Reu, Serug and Nahor. Names that say nothing and mean nothing. Not to us anyway. 'And they had sons and daughters … .' 'So what?' we want to say.

Then suddenly, at the end of the chapter, a name appears: Abraham. A name like the morning star, signalling the end of a long, dark, fearful night. Abraham: a name like a blessing.

The whole history of Abraham is captured in three words: God *speaks*; Abraham *hears*; Abraham *goes*. To where? To a different land, a different city, says the writer of Hebrews; a city of the future. Abraham goes out into the world, to transform the world, to be a vehicle of God's promise – the bearer of God's blessing, the embodiment of God's grace. Abraham does what the tower builders of Babel could not and would not do: he listens to God's voice and is willing to be scattered. He does not stay in Haran, but leaves, without certainties or guarantees, abandoning all that has meaning in terms of cultural and political identity, abandoning the territory of his father's gods, in utter faith and trust in the One who has called him.

And as Abraham, not knowing where he was going, steps outside the walls of his city into the wide open plains, he steps into the wideness of the grace of God, and becomes, by grace and faith, the role model of all who spurn the tower and challenge its power. They speak with a new tongue, fulfilling what God spoke through the prophet,

> At that time I will change the speech of the peoples to
> a pure speech, that all of them may call on the name of
> the LORD and serve him with one accord…
> (Zephaniah 3:9)

Now the unity lies not in the sameness of uniformity, but in the multitudinous praise of the glory of the LORD. Now the speech is not threatening, or cajoling, or manipulative, but *pure*. That is speech beyond the confused babble of Babel, beyond the fearful gibberish of godless humankind, beyond the prideful chatter of the tower builders. It is the speech of those who believe, and 'look forward to the city that has foundations, whose architect and builder is God'. (Hebrews 11:10)

Try God: Be Bold

Then the men set out from there, and they looked toward Sodom; and Abraham went with them to set them on their way. The LORD said, 'Shall I hide from Abraham what I am about to do, seeing that Abraham shall become a great and mighty nation, and all the nations of the earth shall be blessed in him? No, for I have chosen him that he may charge his children and his household after him to keep the way of the LORD by doing righteousness and justice; so that the LORD may bring about for Abraham what he has promised him.' Then the LORD said, 'How great is the outcry against Sodom and Gomorrah and how very grave their sin! I must go down and see whether they have done altogether according to the outcry that has come to me; and if not, I will know.' So the men turned from there, and went toward Sodom, while Abraham remained standing before the LORD. Then Abraham came near and said, 'Will you indeed sweep away the righteous with the wicked?' ... He answered, 'For the sake of ten I will not destroy it.'

Genesis 18:16-23, 32

By all accounts, Genesis 19 is a grim story. It bristles with willful obstinacy and reeks of the deliberate resistance to the will of God. It is aflame with violence and destruction. Yet I have the feeling that, in some strange way, it gives many Christians a good feeling. Especially the second part. The wicked get their just desserts, just the way they should. God punishes sin, and with a vengeance that's second to none. It gives us the feeling that everything is in its right place. It is most comfortable: a God who does what is expected, who conforms so precisely to our expectations.

In this reading, Genesis 18 is no more than a somewhat irritating delay before we get to the real stuff. Abraham is actually wasting God's time – and ours! – by attempting to bargain God down from his position of rightful anger. It is understandable only if one accepts that Abraham's real concern is not Sodom and Gomorrah, but Lot and his family. Then Abraham's point is not the preservation of Sodom and Gomorrah because of the righteous that might be found there, but the safety of his family. There is a collective sigh of relief when that is indeed achieved, but God's justice is not deflected. It is a popular belief, but one that is nonetheless challenged, and is crossed by the Bible itself.

It is a mistake to read Genesis 19 in isolation. Genesis 19 cannot be properly understood without Genesis 18. Abraham's intercessory prayer is more than just a delaying tactic, more than a strategy of the narrator to build up the tension necessary for a good story.

It does raise some preliminary questions though. For instance, if the destruction of Sodom and Gomorrah had been predetermined by God's justice as some are insisting, why pray at all? Or, why bother when the situation is so clear: there is no doubt about the sinfulness of the two cities here. Conversely, if God is a God of mercy, slow to anger and quick to forgive, why does God need to be persuaded? And what is this bargaining thing? Is that not just a bit undignified, for Abraham certainly, but also for God? After all, about the sinfulness of the cities, and therefore their rightful condemnation, there can be no doubt whatsoever.

In the end, the cities are destroyed, Lot and his two daughters are saved, but his wife is left behind as a pillar of salt, which in itself raises a totally different, but in my view devastating question. Not just: why is her looking back regarded as such an unforgivable sin? But: why is the sin of Lot so blithely glossed over? After all, are not Lot's sins in this chapter far more condemnable than hers? There is, I think, an incredible travesty in this. What does one say of a father who does what Lot does in vv. 6, 7, and 8? Who and what is a man who offers his daughters to a raging mob intent on violence and rape? 'Look my brothers,' Lot says, 'I have two daughters who have not slept with a man. Let me bring them out to you and you can do what you like with them.' We speak so glibly of the 'depravity' of the men of Sodom, and correctly so. But what about the depravity of Lot? I do not want to begin to think of what might have gone on in the minds of those two young women as they sat there in that house, listening to the wild beasts outside and hearing the voice of their father.

The shameful acts of the men here warrant a separate sermon. But Abraham prays, and Lot and his two daughters are saved. It is the mother who is punished, because she 'looked back'. So the question is not: 'is intercessory prayer necessary?' but rather 'is it *helpful?*' Abraham prays not for himself or his family, nor for just the righteous who might reside in the two cities. He prays for Sodom and Gomorrah as a whole. For Abraham there is a lot more at stake here than the lot of Lot. These two cities are not just two cities, they are a symbol for the world. The point here is not the sinfulness of two cities, but the *condition of humankind*. What we have learned about Lot should already caution us here. The story of Sodom and Gomorrah does not say, 'There but for the grace of God go I.' The Bible does not allow us the sinful luxury of distancing ourselves from the realities of our own waywardness. The story of Sodom and Gomorrah says, 'This is what we are.' The question Abraham's prayer raises is not whether enough righteous people can be found in Sodom and Gomorrah, but whether it is possible for the righteous to save the world, even if the world is so bent on its own destruction. The issue, therefore, is not whether God can be bargained with. The issue, rather, is the weight of righteousness. How much weight do the righteous put in the scales of God's justice? Is there hope for the world, is the real question.

Believers see themselves as part of that world, not separate from it, although not *of it* but certainly *in it*. For that reason we are responsible for the world in which we live. It is a world created by God for the glory of God, not so that it could be ruled, and finally destroyed, by evil. So for Abraham the issue was not how wonderful it would be for the wicked to be destroyed, but how wonderful if the wicked could be *saved*. If the world is the 'theatre of God's glory' as John Calvin said, then the believer does not wait impatiently for its destruction, but works ceaselessly for its salvation.

This is a long way from the privatised piety which so often permeates and controls our faith and prayer life. In our prayers as well as in our doing of our faith, the concern should not, and cannot, be just ourselves, or the personal things so dear to us. It should be God's world, unrepentant and with its perverse love for self-destruction. *That* should also be our concern. The question is not only, how can *I* be saved, but: is there, for us, for *humanity*, and not just for Christians, in this world, a different way of life, so that we do not destroy ourselves?

II

This much is clear: sin cannot be pooh-poohed or simply prayed away. The sins of Sodom and Gomorrah are 'very grave', and 'the outcry is great' (v. 20). Those who suffer under the sins of Sodom and Gomorrah cry out to God, like the blood of Abel cried out. It is a cry not from the outside, but from the victims of injustice inside the city. The cry is for heavenly judgement, for divine vengeance, for liberation. And that is why Abraham prays with such persistence. The greater the sin, the more passionate the prayer. With us it is often the other way around: the more outrageous the sin, the less enthusiastic our prayers. We write people off, and with an alacrity that often stuns the mind. Yet, God judges not even Sodom and Gomorrah without first having gone 'down' to 'see whether they have done altogether according to the outcry that has come to me' (v. 21). This God will judge no one on hearsay.

It is time to ask the question that's been the back of our minds from the beginning. What then is the sin of Sodom and Gomorrah? The traditional answer, based on more than a century of exegesis of this text, and brought back by popular demand time and time again, is 'homosexuality'. Hence the word 'sodomy' in our dictionaries, inspired by what we believe to have been the despicable acts of the men of Sodom.

But is that so? The problem seems to centre on the words 'to know them' in 19:5. According to traditional, and popular, exegesis, the word 'sodomy' always means 'to have sexual relations'. Accordingly, the NIV, among others, does not hesitate to translate: '... so that we can we have sex with them'. We shall have to take a closer look at this. And please, let us not be in any hurry: too many lives over too many years have been utterly destroyed by our haste to judge. In fact what has been called 'a history of judgement' (referring to the unanimity of biblical scholars on this issue) may well turn out to be a history of pre-judgement!

The word 'to know' (*yadah*) is used no fewer than four times in Genesis 24, and only once refers to sexual relationships. The same word is used in Exodus 33:17, Numbers 14:31, Jeremiah 31:34, and Hosea 6:3. In not one of these texts is the word related to sex. Careful analysis shows that the grievous sin here in Genesis 19 has more to do with breaking the laws of hospitality and of protection (in other words, 'love') which are so central to the godly life in the Hebrew Bible, than with homosexual conduct.

The same is true in Judges 19, an almost similar text, where the desire of the men of Gibeah is not for homosexual relations per se, but rather for any violent deed that would satisfy their utter perverse lust. In the end *their* victims were not the men but the women, and the biblical revulsion is not less, but greater.

The refusal to make a home for strangers, to safeguard them from harm, the violence that bubbles just under the surface and finally, inevitably, breaks out – these are all signs of the total depravity, the inversion of values and the loss of sensitivity for right and wrong that are the hallmark of a people, a community, a world which turns its back on God. The violence can, and often does, include sexual abuse, but is not by any means obviously 'homosexual'.

III

Moreover, the Bible itself tells us what it considers to be 'the sins of Sodom and Gomorrah'. The first reference is Jeremiah 23:14. The context is Jeremiah 22 and 23 where the judgement of the LORD begins with the king who does not know justice:

> Thus says the LORD: Act with justice and
> righteousness, and deliver from the hand of the
> oppressor anyone who has been robbed. And do no
> wrong or violence to the alien, the orphan, and the
> widow, or shed innocent blood in this place. (22:3)

Already the framework for understanding the text is set. The king is told that his father did justice and righteousness, and judged the cause of the poor and needy. 'Is not this to know me? says the LORD.' (v.16)

But it is not only the king upon whose head God's judgement rains. Also the shepherds who 'destroy and scatter the sheep of my pasture' (23:1), as well as the prophets, both in Samaria and Jerusalem:

> … they commit adultery and walk in lies; they
> strengthen the hands of the evildoers, so that no one
> turns from wickedness; all of them have become like
> Sodom to me, and its inhabitants like Gomorrah.
> (vv.14, 15)

As with Sodom and Gomorrah, it is the sinfulness of a whole community, the disobedience of a whole people, that causes the outcry. Yahweh begins with the king, then moves on to the shepherds, then the prophets and the priests, and finally 'all the inhabitants of Jerusalem', for 'from the prophets of Jerusalem ungodliness has spread throughout the land'. (v.15)

Ezekiel is even more explicit, (16:49):

> This was the sin of your sister Sodom: she and her
> daughters had pride, excess of food and prosperous
> ease, but did not aid the poor and the needy. They were
> haughty and did abominable things before me ... .

The sins of Sodom and Gomorrah had to with the lack of justice and the doing of injustice, with lies and adultery and unfaithfulness; with turning away from the poor and needy in haughtiness and pride; with excess of food and that prosperity that comes from robbing the poor. At issue here is a lack of love and a love of violence, not knowing the difference between good and evil.

We might as well forget our smug judgements on 'queers', 'faggots' and 'dykes' at whom we turn up our super-Christian noses. The sins of Sodom and Gomorrah are the condition of all of us who do not do justice, do not feed the hungry, do not aid the needy, do not know mercy and compassion, do not know how to walk humbly with our God. We are all in need of God's grace, love, mercy and forgiveness.

All of a sudden we understand how much, for all of us, there is at stake in Genesis 18 and 19.

IV

The story is not yet over, the Bible is not done with us on this topic yet. Have you noticed just how this whole chapter 18 is permeated with trepidation, how every sentence trembles with a holy hesitation? Abraham's voice shakes with wonder even as he speaks.

> Let me take it upon myself to speak to the LORD,
> I who am but dust and ashes ... .

This he says in verse 27, and again in verse 31. In verse 30 it becomes even clearer: 'Oh do not let the LORD be angry if I speak …', and in verse 31: 'Oh do not let the LORD be angry if I speak just once more … '.

We feel the awe in every word. Abraham knows: I am speaking with the Holy One of Israel. We, with our irritating impatience with all things that go beyond our meagre understanding, with our childish urge to make every unreachable thing accessible, with our banal craving to make all things holy, familiar, have no feeling for this, no understanding for it. We do not know the meaning of respectful distance. But for Israel, it was always thus: Jacob at Bethel, knowing that 'God is in this place', and that 'this is the very gate of heaven'. Moses in his unshod feet before the burning bush, Elijah in the cave in the presence of the silence, Isaiah caught up in his vision, surrounded by the voices of seraphs: 'Holy, holy, holy is the LORD of hosts …'.

And we must dig deeper still, along with the text:

> Will you indeed sweep away the righteous with the wicked?

But in verse 25 Abraham goes further still:

> Far be it from you to do such a thing, to slay the
> righteous with the wicked! Far be it from you! Shall not
> the judge of all the earth do what is just?

Now the awe is filled with a boldness that is quite startling. What Abraham is saying is this: *can* God, *shall* God, if God is God and not some willful, unstable tyrant, destroy two whole cities, just like that? By what logic is this possible? Has God (like humans) fallen helplessly into a cycle of violent retribution and vengeance? For that is the way of the gods of the nations surrounding Israel. But the God of Israel? This God is the 'judge of all the earth'. That has always been Israel's confession. This God's very essence is justice. 'All his ways are just' sings the hymn of Deuteronomy 32, therefore 'He is the Rock, a faithful God who does no wrong, upright and just is he.' Not to do justice is so alien to Yahweh as to be impossible and unthinkable.

> When Yahweh judges the world, the world will be
> judged in righteousness and with justice. (Psalms 9:8)

How can God, Abraham is saying, suddenly live in denial of what God truly is? Not to heed the righteousness of the righteous, and to be swayed only by the sins of the wicked, and as a result to destroy the world, is the essence of injustice, and that, Abraham says, is impossible. As God calls Israel to do justice, so Abraham calls upon God: 'Do justice!' And he poses a rhetorical question which God cannot but answer in the affirmative: 'Shall not the judge of all the earth do what is just?'

It is not true, Abraham argues, that the holiness of God demands the vengeance of God. Rather the holiness of God demands mercy and forgiveness. Abraham finds it impossible to believe that a holy, just God can destroy the world because of the unjust, and *despite* the presence of the righteous. It is not the unjust that should cause the destruction of the world; rather, the just should guarantee the life of the world. Like Moses would do much later, Abraham is reminding God of who God is, reminding God of God's promises. You gave these people your promise, Moses says, you cannot fail us now. Abraham is just as adamant: it is your desire for life that makes you God, not the lust for punishment. You are God, the Living One – be it! Distinguish yourself from the lifeless gods of the earth, over whom you pass judgement.

What staggering boldness, what faith! It is a boldness that comes because of the fear of the LORD. The words 'far be it from you!' are sometimes read as a plea. I read it as a bold reminder to God, a statement of trust, a confession of faith. Thus speaks a person who truly knows God. And this is why Abraham is called 'the father of the faithful'.

V

But we understand Abraham's boldness truly only when we read the Bible more closely. The true shocker is in verse 22:

> ... but Abraham remained standing before the Lord ... .

That is how just about all translations read. But the Hebrew text itself leans more toward another reading:

> … but the LORD remained standing before Abraham … .

I believe this to be the correct translation. But this translation proved too much for our translators. It goes too far, for the implication is, Abraham is calling God to account, Abraham has God on the carpet! Abraham is refusing to let God go until he has spoken his piece. And here's the thing: God stands there, listening, responding. Willing to wait until Abraham is done.

The mind boggles. As it should. We are totally stunned by this boldness. Abraham does something we would not have held possible, or seemly. Even as we think this, though, we suspect that our false modesty is more a sign of our paucity of faith, than of holy respect. But the question is not: what manner of man is this? But rather: what kind of *God* is this? And this is the source of the hesitation we detect in the text. This is, indeed, holy ground. It is the very edge, as far as human beings dare to go. But it is the daring not out of arrogance or hubris or ignorance. It is the daring of true faith. It is the boldness of this faith that brings us so close to the heart of God. And it is that closeness which makes us tremble. And Abraham knows it:

> Oh, let the LORD not be angry if I speak … .

Some say: the holiness of God demands holy vengeance. Abraham says: the holiness of God demands divine mercy.

Some say: the sins of the world dishonour God; God has no choice, the world must perish – let the floods return! Oh, the righteous do their best, but the guilt of the wicked weighs so much more. Abraham says: it cannot be that there is no hope for the world, just because there is so much sin. For if God is anything, God is more than our sins.

But nothing is taken for granted here. Neither the righteousness of the righteous, nor the mercy of God. That is why Abraham 'bargains', and trembles as he does so. And that is why God responds. The reality of sin, judgement, and mercy that counts our sins for naught and grants us righteousness, always brings us to this point. But it takes a boldness born of faith to discover this.

The question is: who will dare to call upon God like this? Who will be bold enough to try God? Our world is dying; we are engulfed by war and rumours of war and once again the strong is rattling the sabres at the weak and the foolish. Our political discourse is lies and hypocrisy, our daily bread is lovelessness and alienation, and civility is for the fainthearted. We bow down at the altars of the gods of godlessness, on which we sacrifice both the poor and our faith.

Who will call God to account? Who will dare to ask God to be God? Who will dare to ask what weighs heavier: the sins of the millions, or the righteousness of ten? Who will, with trembling and faith, intercede with God for the world? If we are willing to try God, we will discover, with Abraham, that there is hope for the world. That it is true: the presence, the hope, the faith, the love, the obedience of only ten, can change the lot of the world.

But God, as always, is already ahead of us. Abraham counts till ten. God, when it comes right down to it, counts only to one. And this One, the Righteous One, who knew no sin, 'was made to be sin for our sake, so that in him we might become the righteousness of God' (2 Corinthians 5:21). On Calvary all the sins of the world were laid upon him. He carried, in his dying body, all that dishonours God, and his blood justifies us. And it is upon his righteousness that we stand when we, like Abraham, approach God. His love and sacrifice are the grounds for our boldness. His mercy is an open invitation: try God, be bold!

The Blessed One of the LORD

Now there was a famine in the land, besides the former
famine that had occurred in the days of Abraham. And
Isaac went to Gerar, to King Abimelech of the Philistines.
The LORD appeared to Isaac and said, 'Do not go
down to Egypt; settle in the land that I shall show you.
Reside in this land as an alien, and I will be with you, and
will bless you; for to you and to your descendants I will
give all these lands, and I will fulfil the oath that I swore
to your father Abraham. I will make your offspring as
numerous as the stars of heaven, and will give to your
offspring all these lands; and all the nations of the earth
shall gain blessing for themselves through your offspring,
because Abraham obeyed my voice and kept my
charge, my commandments, my statutes and my laws.'
So Isaac settled in Gerar … From there he went up to
Beersheba. And that very night the LORD appeared
to him and said, 'I am the God of your father Abraham;
do not be afraid, for I am with you and will bless you,
and make your offspring numerous for my servant
Abraham's sake … They said, 'We see plainly that the
LORD has been with you … you are now the blessed
of the LORD'.

Genesis 26:1-6, 23-24, 29

3

Abraham, Isaac and Jacob. That's the way we read it, recite it, remember it. The history of God with Israel begins with the patriarchs, Abraham, Isaac and Jacob. The three bright, shining stars in the firmament of Israel's dawn. The God of Israel is, first and foremost, the God of Abraham, Isaac and Jacob. The promises that are the hope and sustenance of Israel have first been given to Abraham, Isaac and Jacob. The three of them. And yet, if we read carefully and honestly, we discover that Isaac's star shines not nearly as bright. Not as bright as his father's, and not as bright as his son's.

We know Isaac as the long awaited, precious son of Abraham and Sarah, and the deceived, confused and hapless father of Esau and Jacob. Next to the towering figures of his father and his son, Isaac shrivels like a shallow-rooted plant in the burning desert sun. While Abraham and Jacob lived lives of sweeping, high drama, Isaac seems to have lived a life of quiet desperation, uncertainty and internalised pain.

Son of Laughter is the title of a captivating book on Isaac, by pastor/author Frederick Buechner. In his book Buechner paints Isaac's life as tinged by the paradox that dogs Isaac till the end. Actually how much laughter, and what kind of laughter, was there in the life of the son of laughter?

Isaac's life strikes us as unremarkable. No dramatic interfaces with God, no bold intercessory moments, no wrestling until the light of dawn, no dreams under the night sky, far from home on the way to nowhere. Isaac is a plain and simple man who misses the startling intimacy with God that Abraham seemed to have had, and misses also the almost sassy attitude Jacob shows in his relationship with God. In Genesis, fourteen chapters are devoted to Abraham, and from chapter 27 onwards, up to chapter 35, we have what is called the Jacob cycle. Then, beginning at chapter 37, with the exception of chapter 38, follows the Joseph cycle until chapter 50, and even there Jacob features strongly. Even in chapter 22, where Isaac's life is at stake, the point of the story is not the life of Isaac, but the faith of Abraham.

So the question becomes unavoidable: why does the Bible keep on talking about *three* patriarchs? What is it that makes Isaac one? What is Isaac's legacy to the life of Israel and the faithful who would come to believe in the God of Abraham, Isaac and Jacob?

Abraham is called 'the friend of God'. Jacob becomes 'Israel', the one who 'wrestled with God and won'. And Isaac? He remains 'the son of laughter'. At the announcement of his birth Sarah 'laughs to herself' (18:12) and still today there are disputes over whether the meaning of the laughter in 21:6 is 'with me' or 'at me', and in chapter 27:33 the emotion that causes Isaac to 'tremble violently' is far from laughter. Abraham and Jacob evoke strong emotions of admiration, even envy; Isaac elicits our sympathy. We feel for him. 'He was no King Arthur,' one commentator writes of Isaac, 'he was the ordinary son of the extraordinary father [who] never moved out of his narrow little circle in Palestine', a 'passive follower', not a 'commander of men' like his father. What was fine in him developed because 'he had the wisdom and grace to welcome the best that he had inherited …'. In other words, what saved Isaac were his genes, not so much his achievements. Such are the condescending tones in which they speak of Isaac.

Yet the Bible is insistent: 'Abraham, Isaac and Jacob …'.

II

But why? Isaac does not bring anything new to the story. The scholars are careful to point that out. His history merely echoes that of his father. Like Abraham, Isaac experiences famine. And even here the writer himself has to go to some trouble to make the point that he is telling us of Isaac, not Abraham. Like his mother Sarah, his wife Rebekha's beauty elicited unwanted lust from strangers and he, like his father before him, also pretended that she was his sister. The story of the wells follows that of his father closely, as does the incident with King Abimelech. There seem to be no differences, no surprises. Or are there?

There is one big difference between Abraham and Isaac. Abraham's whole life is dominated by two words: *wayalek* and *wayomer*. In the Hebrew these two words belong together, not just through the similarity of sound, but also in the cause and effect they represent. God *spoke* and Abraham *went*. In Genesis 12 Yahweh speaks, and Abraham goes – away from his land, his people, his culture, his gods, his father's house. With Isaac, it is just the opposite. God *speaks*, Isaac *stays*.

This is crucial in our understanding of this underestimated and undervalued man. I think the commentaries have it by the wrong end. It is not so much that Abraham had a 'wide orbit' and Isaac a 'narrow' one. It is not that Abraham 'belonged to the company of the daring' while stodgy Isaac 'energises below his maximum, behaves below his optimum'. If, in his daring to leave, Abraham was driven by a 'higher force', then Isaac, in his staying, was no less driven by the divine will. If the challenge for Abraham to leave was great, the challenge for Isaac to stay was no less great. If God had a reason for Abraham to go, God had a reason for Isaac to stay. If it was Abraham's destiny to go, it was Isaac's destiny to remain, to settle. Follow me on this one.

What does it mean that Isaac has to stay? Has Isaac 'arrived'? Have God's promises been fulfilled? Has the great destiny been reached? Does the history of Yahweh with Israel end here, in this place, this strange land where Yahweh is not known, not honoured, not served, nor worshipped?

No, listen closely: 'Do not go down to Egypt ... ,' Yahweh says, 'settle in the land ... '. But, Yahweh adds, 'reside in this land *as an alien* ... '.

Isaac has to stay, but not as one who has arrived, nor as one who belongs, but as an *alien*: without guarantees and without rights. Tolerated but never accepted. With land on loan, but never owned, at least not in his lifetime. Land to live on, but never to call home. Live there, Yahweh says, but never be at home there. There are no certainties, only the promise. 'I will be with you, and bless you; for to you and to your descendants I will give all these lands, and I will fulfill the oath that I swore to your father Abraham' (26:3,4). Just how difficult that will prove to be we shall discover shortly.

So Isaac settled in Gerar. In obedience to God.

Abraham was called to go. Isaac was called to stay. In this land where no one believed, knew or wanted to know, he was called to stay and to believe, to live from the promises of Yahweh. He has to stay in a land where he did not belong, where no one wanted him, to keep the light burning for future generations, to lay claim on the promises of God for the sake of his children, and his children's children. To believe, for *their* sake, that Yahweh's promises will be fulfilled. He has to stay, so that others may see what faith really is. And inherit the promise.

That, I suggest, is no mean thing.

In verse two, out of nowhere, Egypt is mentioned. Someone must have mentioned Egypt as a possibility. Or Isaac must have weighed Egypt as an option to escape the famine. Egypt, superpower, the land of wealth, of opportunity and safety from hunger. To find refuge there was the obviously sensible thing to do. Looking around him, Isaac thought, Egypt has to be better. Going to Egypt would be the responsible thing to do. But Yahweh is emphatic: 'Do *not* go down to Egypt … .' Almost before Isaac could formulate the thought, argue the point, Yahweh cuts him off. Egypt is not an option. Forget it.

Egypt is not the answer. It is not your place of safety. Egypt is not your sanctuary. Egypt, as good as it may *sound*, is not your future, nor that of your children. God sees what Isaac does not yet see. Egypt *sounds* alright, but beware! Egypt will become a land for slaves, a land of pain and persecution, a land of imprisonment and degradation. Egypt is not *your* land of opportunity; it will become your land of oppression. Now it is land where food is plenty, but it will become the land where the plagues will fall. Where dreams die.

Yahweh sees what Isaac does not see, and says, 'Stay here.' Alone, with your uncertainties, but with your faith. Stay here, with nothing but the dream of God. Stay here, with only the promises of God as your surety. And Isaac believes. And he stays. Alone with his faith, alone with God's promises only he can see. With God's dream only he can read. A stranger in a strange land. An alien with a promise.

The ministry can be a lonely business. The worst loneliness, I think, is not that people leave one on one's own. Often the contrary is true: they encircle you, enclose you, engulf you. The worst is when you alone can see what God sees, when it takes so very long to convince them. When there is no one who shares your vision. When you know there is a promise, but only you can see it is God's promise that will surely be fulfilled.

Elijah stands alone before Ahab and Jezebel, and he is alone in his confrontation with the prophets of Baal. And after that confrontation, when the reaction sets in and he, fearing for his life flees from the wrath of Jezebel, is still utterly alone. He flees from Jezebel, because she is now seeking his life, and he flees from his people for among them he finds no refuge. They saw what he had done at Mount Carmel, and yet they do not surround him with love and protection. It might even be, as it so often is, that his very success against the power of the throne that makes him a hero, is the success that now makes him a pariah. Because they fear Ahab and Jezebel, they dare not be seen with him. Their fear of the throne is greater than their pride in, and gratitude for, Elijah's victory. The depression that sends him into the wilderness to hide under that broom tree is not just the inevitable 'comedown' from the incredible 'high' on the mountain. It is the result of that sense of abandonment that he felt after the empowerment of being 'with the people'. Twice he reveals the core of his misery: 'I alone am left', he confesses to the LORD.

I know that God has to remind him of the fact that he is in fact not alone: that there are seven thousand in Israel left by the LORD, 'all the knees that have not bowed to Baal'. That is true, because God said so. But the question is: *where were they when Elijah needed them most?* No wonder the Bible tells us that he lay himself down 'under a solitary broom tree'. The solitariness of that tree is as poignant as the loneliness of the prophet.

III

As a stranger in that land Isaac's life is not easy. His wife's beauty causes him problems and leads him into the same temptation of weakness his father displayed on this point. There is a chronic shortage of food and the famine brings all sorts of tensions. We become aware of the continuous struggle for survival and the problems around the wells speak volumes. The names actually say it all: *Esek*, 'because they contended with him'; *Sitnah*, 'and they quarrelled over that one also' (26:20, 21). That they did not quarrel over the next one was an enormous relief, and that relief and gratitude too, are reflected in the name: *Rehoboth*, 'Now the LORD has made room for us' (v.22). And when he arrives at Beersheba, as far away from the conflict situation as possible, Yahweh has to assure him: 'Do not be afraid, for I am with you … ' (v.24).

Through it all, this part of the story tells us something about Isaac's character, and his faith. He is not a contentious man. The LORD blesses him, he becomes a man of wealth. His flocks increase, and so does his household, making him the object of envy and jealousy. The Philistines hate him. So much so that Abimelech, who can no longer defend his protection of this alien in the face of the agitation among his subjects, has to send him away. He has become 'too powerful' (26:12-16). The human condition asserts itself: even the blessings from the LORD become a cause of danger. The Philistines may have deemed him powerful, but his power did not secure his strength, it emphasised his vulnerability. Isaac is forced to move toward the valley. He is prepared to move rather than stay and fight. His blessings have made him powerful, but he humbles himself and moves, rather than picking a fight. Have we ever considered what strength of character it must have taken to deny that power, and step away?

The wells he dug were not new; they were the wells his father had dug in his day. Again, in a fit of envy and blind fury, they had been stopped with earth by the Philistines, in the process making it impossible for themselves to use the precious water. Cutting off their noses to spite their faces. This was an act of such mindless stupidity that the narrator feels a need to mention it twice. More than anything this tells us just how unwelcome Isaac had been in the land where he was called to stay. As he begins to start all over again and to open up those wells in order to secure his survival and that of his whole clan, he is dogged by the grim, obtrusive obstreperousness of the Philistines. As he opens up a well, they are there to claim it. 'The water is ours' (v.20). Never mind that his dad had dug the well long ago. But, instead of fighting, he steps back. Instead of standing on his rights, he leaves. Instead of counterclaiming, he quietly moves away. He makes room, again and again, *for others*. He moves from site to site, digging another well each time, until they no longer quarrel any more, and until Yahweh makes room for *him*. Rehoboth: enlargement. Until he comes to a place, in the land and in his life, where he need not fear anymore. Beersheba: his fear is banished; he is not. The promise lives.

Isaac moves away, avoids confrontation, shuns the fight. Was he weak? A pious coward who failed to 'stand up for the LORD'? There are those who suggest that. I don't think so. Isaac moves away, but not from the land, merely to another place. The Philistines want him gone, he just settles elsewhere. He is not boastfully proud, but he is quietly determined. If he had fought he would have risked banishment from the land altogether, and so risk also jeopardising God's dream, to scupper God's plans, to undermine God's promise. What the Philistines see as cowardly bending to their bullying and we modern, militant Christian soldiers as wimpish, is actually the gift of wisdom. Isaac knows: even the essentials of life such as water are not worth sacrificing the dream of God for. Isaac picks his battles, and his battleground. Isaac knows: God has something else in store, the dream lives, the promise remains. Isaac is convinced: the dream is greater than his own pride. Isaac believes: it *shall* come to pass. I find that quite amazing.

And I believe I know from experience just how incredibly hard that is. The past ten years have brought me to many places where I knew: this is a well I have dug. I have made the sacrifices, I have given leadership, I have held on to the promise in dark and difficult times. I have inspired others with it. I have put my life on the line for it. But someone else has claimed the water. I had to make a decision: I could remain the man of old, or I could become like Isaac, making place for God to fight my battles for me. I could stand on my pride and my achievements, claiming my rightful reward, or I could learn to trust God with all of my life. I could resist, claim my rights and defend myself, or I could move on, making room for others, knowing that God would bring me to a place, the *right* place, where God himself would make room for me. I made room, and I believe passionately that the time will come when the well God has chosen for me will give water, a Rehoboth, a place of enlargement and freedom from fear. I know it will come. God will enlarge my dreams. He will enlarge my hopes. He will enlarge my future. He will enlarge my life. But let me not bluff you: it is hard. It takes grace. It takes mercy. It takes more than what you have within yourself.

IV

If people should ask us about our faith, our ministry, our calling, we really would like to say we feel like Abraham, called and ready to leave behind the known for the unknown, the certainties for the uncertain future, with our faith in God as our guide – no maps, no guarantees. Or maybe we would like to be compared to Jacob: we wrestled with God and we were victorious, staying in that battle until the morning light, not letting go until we were blessed. How we would like to testify that we have fought and won; that we are now walking with a limp, but we are walking towards the fulfilment of the promises of God.

But in truth we are far more like the Isaac we knew before we heard this sermon. A stranger in a strange land, more confused than wise, more in the margins than on centre page, more down in the dumps than high on the mountain. I am talking to ministers of the gospel here; you *know* what I am talking about.

The evil we did not do we are accused of anyway; the good we try to do is not seen nor mentioned. Sometimes the ministry is far more battlefield than place of peace; far more waters of discontent than well of inspiration. Preparing our sermons for every Sunday becomes a struggle; we worry about having to say the same words differently, wondering whether they will fall on fertile ground, whether we can still, or ever, make a difference. We suspect that the flatness of the worship service is merely an echo of the shallowness of our own declining spirituality. We wrestle with our own unbelief and we are afraid of what the people might suspect.

Often we are torn apart by the unholy paradoxes that plague the ministry. People insist on the grace of God while they themselves show so little of the mercy that is demanded from God. The forgiveness they expect from God breaks apart on the rocks of their own unforgiving nature. And sometimes the chasm between the command to love and the church's own lovelessness tends to drive us crazy. And it all comes down on your head.

Sometimes we experience the church as Isaac did his search for water: signs along the roads of our pain. We stagger from Esek to Sitnah and pray for Rehoboth: 'Please make room for us!' We struggle with evil and feel totally powerless. We struggle with the small-mindedness of people and that totally discourages us. We struggle with the incomprehensibility of the ways of God and that totally diminishes us. Our prayers taste like sand, the bread of communion like stones and the wine like vinegar.

We are not like Abraham but like Isaac and the temptation just to get out and away from it all is sometimes too much to bear. It is more prevalent than we are sometimes willing to admit. Some of us stay in the ministry simply because we are not trained for anything else that's useful. Speaking with a friend about my desire to return to the ministry, his response was: 'Why are you trying so hard to get back in, while most of us are trying so hard to get out?'

V

And then comes the voice of God: stay here, in your ministry, in my work, as an alien; but an alien with a promise. Seek justice, not popularity. Seek peace, not just accommodation to hardship. Seek to give leadership, not just lessons in survival. Seek, and bring, hope when hopelessness reigns. Seek genuine love when hatred is such an easy way out. Seek genuine reconciliation when cheap grace is such a temptation. Seek to speak the truth in love, when silence is so much the easier option. Believe in God's divine purpose for your life, even though you might not always understand the ways of God with your life. Cling to God's promises even though you might not get rich from it. Make room for others, even adversaries, believing that God will enlarge your own life in his own time. There is a future, a destiny, if you can but see it. And remember always that we do what we do for the sake of Jesus.

If we do this, the world will be forced to recognise what Abimelech had to acknowledge: 'You are now the blessed one of the LORD.' The 1953 Afrikaans translation suggests – and correctly so, I think – 'You are the one whom the LORD has blessed (and there is nothing we can do but to acknowledge it).' Isaac hears this, despite the pain in his life, despite his sorrow about his brother Ishmael, despite his wife, who together with his son Jacob so shamelessly deceived him, despite his difficult struggle to remain faithful to the call of God.

The world can do what it likes – *you* are the blessed one of God. Satan can aim all his deadly arrows at you – *you* are the blessed one of God. You might get tired of the struggle and weary of making room for others while you are constantly backed into a corner – *you* are the blessed one of God. You might be dismayed by your failures and disheartened by your shortcomings – you *are* the blessed one of God. And the world will have to acknowledge it, just as Abimelech had to. Of all the accolades a preacher can get: talented teacher, gifted preacher, accomplished administrator, empathetic pastor, great counsellor – the greatest of all is when we can be called the blessed one of God.

VI

The words I think are the most encouraging, the most inspiring, are found at the end of the chapter. Isaac's servants come to give him the good news: 'We have found water' (v. 32). The struggle, the pain, the suffering; it has all been worth it. The strife and conflict, withstanding the temptation to prove himself, just once, has all been worth it. Holding on when there was nothing tangible to hold onto. Believing the unseen when everybody else dealt only with what could be seen, reaching for the promise only he could see, on behalf of generations yet unborn – it's all worth it. They have found water.

And that is the ultimate reward. That people, through our ministry, our faith, our faithfulness, would discover that their lives have changed, that we have made a difference, that we have helped them see beyond what was immediate and tangible. That through our ministry they have glimpsed the vision of God, they have seen the promise, they have believed. They have found water.

No, there is good reason why Isaac is included: Isaac, son of laughter. No, no, not the laughter of comic relief or derision, but the sound of heavenly joy in the strength and faith of a favourite son who believed in the promise. Isaac, an ancestor of faith, a keeper of the promise, a seer of things unseen, a shining star in the firmament of God, the blessed one of the LORD.

A Word to the Living

Moses convened all Israel, and said to them: 'Hear, O
Israel, the statutes and ordinances that I am addressing
to you today; you shall learn them and observe them
diligently. The LORD our God made a covenant with us
at Horeb. Not with our ancestors did the LORD make
this covenant, but with us, who are all of us alive here
today. The LORD spoke with you face to face at the
mountain, out of the fire. (At that time I was standing
between the LORD and you to declare to you the
words of the LORD; for you were afraid because of the
fire and did not go up the mountain.) And he said: 'I am
the LORD your God, who brought you out of the land
of Egypt, out of the house of slavery; you shall have no
other gods before me ... If only they had such a mind
as this, to fear me and to keep my commandments
always, so that it might go well with them and with their
children for ever!'

Deuteronomy 5:1-6, 29

4

I

We do not know when, where, or by whom exactly the book of Deuteronomy was written. Our best guess is the time of the latter kings and that it was written by one or more authors. What is clear, however, is that Deuteronomy was written for an Israel in crisis: a divided land, divided kingdom, divided people, divided worship, divided loyalties, divided hearts. This book is presented as the last, passionate sermons of Moses and the words of Deuteronomy are intended to speak with the heavy weight of his authority.

But, by the time the people hear these words, Moses' great fear that they would not heed the covenant had come to pass. The people missed their calling; Israel could not resist the overwhelming presence of the cults and culture of Canaan. They were stung, then shocked, then tempted and finally seduced by the sheer visibility of the gods of the promised land. This issue of visibility was one of the biggest problems that Israel faced. In Canaan, every need had created its own god: for rain, fertility, war – the list is long. And for every god there was a dedicated temple with an image, made by human hands, depicting the presence and the power of that god. Israel could have none of this; it served a God whose law was clear, of which Deuteronomy was a persistent reminder: 'You shall have no other gods before me. You shall not make for yourself an idol … .' (vv.7, 8) All Israel had, Deuteronomy acknowledges, is 'the voice'. 'You heard the sound of words, but saw no form; there was only a voice' (4:12). It must have been difficult indeed to explain this in a culture where a visible, touchable presence was everything. And it must have been harder still to defend.

They were once people of the desert and of the land, with a strong sense of community and solidarity, with strong leaders who had walked in the presence of God. That generation of leaders was now gone, and so was that peculiar closeness to the God of the exodus and the wilderness. The experience of feeling the whip of the slave driver, facing the wrath of a pharaoh who, despite his own power as a reigning god in the most advanced empire on earth, had to acknowledge the power of a God of slaves; the experience of the splitting of the waters and the death of evil upon the seashore; of a cloud by day and a pillar of fire by night; of manna from heaven and water out of a rock; of fire and thunder and a radiant Moses with stone tablets in his hands, trembling still from having been in the presence of the Holy One – all this was ancient history now. It may all have been true but, if so, it was true for another generation, a long dead generation, far removed from this new reality.

This reality was different. They were no longer in Egypt, or in the desert, all on their own. They were in a new land, and had been in fact, for a long time. They were now surrounded by peoples far more sophisticated than they, with gorgeous temples and impressive statues of their gods. Here indeed, a whole generation grew up, knowing nothing about the great deeds of Yahweh, the God of Israel. They felt removed, no, *alienated* from this invisible God, and from a mountain they no longer saw; from a promise they could no longer interpret or believe in, from a covenant made with dead people, whose relevance to their situation they could not fathom.

They, a blessed nation, called to be a blessing to the whole world? A world that had fought them, conquered them, exiled them and now could afford to ignore them? A world that could not care one way or the other whether it received such a blessing or not? In their divided and fallen state, they could not be a blessing to themselves, let alone to the world! What Isaac had inherited from Abraham, and heard from God as an everlasting promise, that 'through your offspring, all nations on earth will be blessed' (Gen. 26:4) must to them have sounded like some cruel, cosmic joke.

It was for such a time that Deuteronomy was written, recalling those great sermons of Moses as he reviewed his forty years as leader of the people, and as he saw them moving into, and taking their place in the promised land. In the face of this divisiveness, the alienation and uncertainty, comes the reminder of the covenant Yahweh had made with Israel. In contrast with the multi-faceted reality of Canaanite religiosity comes the proclamation of the oneness and uniqueness of the revelation of God: *one* LORD, *one* land of promise, *one* Torah, *one* place of worship, *one* people, *one* covenant.

II

Israel must, under these circumstances, hear anew the covenant, the commandments, the 'words'. It is not just mere repetition, but a new proclamation of the liberating deeds of Yahweh, of the uniqueness of this God, and the uniqueness of God's people.

'*Shema Yisrael!*' Hear, o Israel! It is a call reminiscent of the thunder that the people once heard on that unforgettable day at the mountain. A call that is rooted in the inalienable proclamation of freedom: 'I am the LORD your God. I brought you out of the land of Egypt.' Throughout the whole book, the people hearing these words now, are reminded that these are the words their God spoke to Moses. 'These are the words ...' (1:1); 'This is the law ...' (4:44); 'These are the commandments ...' (6:1); 'These are the entire commandments ...' (8:1); 'These are the statutes and ordinances ...' (12:1); 'These are the words ...' (29:1); and then in 33:1, summing it up, focusing on the innermost meaning of it all, revealing the deepest intentions of Yahweh, 'This is the blessing ... '.

'*Shema Yisrael!*' Hear these words, accept them, own them, believe them, live them, stand by them, fall by them – for without them there is no hope, no life, no future, no humaneness, no freedom. Over against the condition of slavery and inhumanity in Egypt stands not the promised land, but the proclamation of the Torah. The freedom of God's people is not guaranteed by entering the promised land, but by accepting and obeying the Torah. '*Shema Yisrael!*' These are the words of the covenant. And it is not just a 'contract', a 'legal arrangement' between God and God's people just like an arrangement between a king and his vassal. It is, let me say it again, the proclamation of freedom: the freedom of Yahweh to do great things for Israel, and the freedom for Israel to respond with love and obedience and boldness. The covenant rests on the Ten Words, but the Ten Words rest on the proclamation of liberation from Egypt, and nowhere is it made as clear as in Deuteronomy. The covenant is not a legal proclamation awaiting a legalistic response; it is freedom calling forth freedom.

The Covenant proclaims: 'I am the LORD your God, who brought you out of the land of Egypt, out of the house of slavery ... '.

The Covenant affirms: 'I am your God, and you shall be my people ... '.

The Covenant declares: 'Whoever calls upon the name of the LORD, shall be saved ... '.

The Covenant promises: 'Therefore the LORD impatiently waits to be gracious unto you, for the LORD is a God of justice; blessed are all who wait for Him ... '.

The Covenant upholds: 'If my people, who are called by my name, humble themselves, pray, seek my face and turn away from their wicked ways, I shall forgive them and heal their land ...'.

The Covenant pleads: 'Remember that you were a slave in Egypt, but the LORD your God redeemed you ... He brought you out of Egypt with his own presence, by his great power – there is no one besides him ...'.

The Covenant demands: 'Let justice roll down like waters, and righteousness like a mighty stream ...'.

The Covenant reminds: 'What does the LORD require of you, but to do justice, to love mercy and to walk humbly with your God ...'.

And this covenant, says Deuteronomy, is made, not with some far-off, long-gone generation, but with us. This is one of the clear indications that this book was in fact written long after Moses, for a generation that had forgotten who they were, where they had come from; who must be told 'not to forget' the road they have travelled. The point the writer wants to make is emphatic. The covenant is a covenant *for today*. It is not outdated or irrelevant, it speaks with the same power; it is as redemptive now as it was then.

We should hear these words as that first congregation heard them:

> Not with our ancestors, but with us, who are all of us
> here alive today.

If the English translation sounds somewhat clumsy, it is because the Hebrew is so emphatic. The Hebrew uses no less than seven words, heaped upon one another – seven times, a number to remember, a sacred count, a number that expresses the fullness of God's intentions, the full weight of God's affirmation:

> Not with our ancestors, but with us, we, these ones,
> here, today, all of us, living.

We must allow that to sink in so that we too, can feel the full weight of these words, move with the rhythm of them, savour the taste of them, be uplifted by the swell of them.

We need not only to understand them, we truly *need* them. To know, to live.

III

To some in that congregation, this might not have sounded very uplifting at all. They might have thought that sermon blatantly unfair. After all, they might say, our situation is so much different, so much more complex. It's so much easier to love God in the desert where there is hardly anyone else to love, where one's options are so obviously limited; to depend on God's providence when you're hungry, to believe when Moses takes all responsibility on himself anyway.

We are surrounded by temptations, tempted by gods, challenged by beliefs and philosophies and ideas not even Moses knew! We are confronted with centuries-old civilizations whose explanations of things make eminent sense. We are not in the desert, all on our own, we have other nations in the immediate vicinity against whom we are being measured and, to be quite honest, we don't always come out so well. When one is in the desert, it is easy to believe in one's uniqueness, or the uniqueness of one's God. When one sees the achievements of others, listens to their histories, sees their military and technological prowess, one's own uniqueness comes across as just a little arrogant. In pluralistic Canaan 'uniqueness' just does not fly.

Besides, it is so much easier when there is strong, decisive leadership; people who knew God and who could set an example! Look at the wimps and hypocrites *we* have to be content with: an Ahab instead of a Moses, a Jeroboam instead of a Joshua, a Jezebel instead of a Miriam. To say nothing of that long line of kings of whom just about every prophet complained that they 'did what was evil in the eyes of Yahweh'.

And why are *we* accused of disobedience and faithlessness, as if *we* were the only culprits around here? It's really been a long process of decay, if one is but honest enough to admit and recognize it. After all, it's true: Jeroboam did make those golden calves and set them up in temples to rival the one in Jerusalem: Dan and Bethel. He *did* call on the people to bow down before them, and he did say, 'Here are your gods, o Israel, who led you out of the land of Egypt!' And it's also true: Jehoram, son of Ahab, followed his example, but hey! Who did it first? Was it not Aaron, that priest of the first hour, with Egypt's memory still fresh in their minds, and right under Moses' nose too? They did not even have the excuse of time and distance, like we do.

It all sounds so persuasively plausible, so justifiably arguable, so devastatingly logical – and so depressingly familiar. Indeed, there is a whole new generation who knows nothing of the great deeds of God and understands nothing about the covenant.

IV

Talk of the covenant embarrasses us, so much so that we have left it to the right-wing religious fundamentalists, as we have done with so much of the Christian faith. Its honesty about sin and faithlessness and its openness about God's love and faithfulness, our need for repentance and forgiveness, offend us. Our talk about justice has been relegated to departmental reports at Synod and to somewhat vague discussions with the 'Justice Desk' at the Council of Churches. In Western theological discourse we have spent the last half-century creating theologies which avoid addressing God, becoming far more adept at psycho-babble about God. And in South Africa we are so keen at political correctness that we are in real danger of replacing the imperatives from the gospel with the demands of culture. We echo the already empty echoes about 'family values' from the TBN Channel and we watch *Oprah* for tips on counselling. So what can we say about a covenant with God? A covenant that calls for a prophetic presence in the world – how can we speak of it when the church in this country has become so curiously and embarrassingly silent on public issues? When we hardly give leadership to God's people on the myriad issues that arise in our new democracy? When we are still struggling to find words of compassion and justice for Aids victims, while six hundred die of the disease in this country *every day*?

And so, once again, the church is on sale. Precious truths paid for by the death of Christ and the sacrifices of the martyrs are once again going at basement bargain prices: peace, truth, reconciliation, faith, compassion, love, justice. Who would have thought that the church, called into being by the One who loved the world so much that He gave his only begotten Son, would become this lifeless, loveless, uncaring insiders' club?

Who would have guessed that the church, named for the One who opened the gates of God's kingdom to the poor, the weak, the rejected and despised, the maimed, the blind and the trod-upon, would become so exclusive, so hypocritical, so closed, racist and oppressive?

Who would have believed that the church, built on the faith of Mary, the confession of Martha, the witness of Mary Magdalene, and the apostolic labour of Junia would become so hard, so chauvinistic, so sinfully patriarchal?

Who could have imagined that the church, which bears the name of him who said, 'Love your enemies', and 'Put up your sword', would devise a 'theology of just war', bless battleships, pray over bombs, bend the knee before politicians who justify the murder of children?

Who could have dreamed that the church, raised on the words of Jesus, the preaching of Paul, and the teaching of Priscilla would be turned, seduced and silenced by a different gospel, led by the nose to a conservative agenda that claims the gospel yet reflects so little of the gospel?

Who could have known that we, who have been given the keys of the kingdom, would ourselves remain locked out, because we would prevent so many from getting in?

And who would have believed that God would be so gracious, so loving as to forgive our sins, blot out our transgressions, strengthen us in our weakness, call us again and again from the darkness into the light; empower us to speak, loving us into becoming children of God? Making of us, in spite of ourselves, the church of Jesus Christ?

Confronted with the ramifications of our own forgetfulness, we are a generation without words but, because of the love of Christ, not without a future.

V

It is for a time like this that Deuteronomy was written. It is for a time like this that Deuteronomy must be preached. It is time to reclaim the covenant for us, the living. We are speaking of God's covenant, not the sterile repetition of meaningless rules and regulations; not predictable shouts of hell and damnation, fire and brimstone; not the gleeful arrest and vengeful suppression of human freedom, or a new legalism which forgets that Paul exhorted us not to become 'slaves of humans'. Not the exhortations of unimaginative religiosity, nor the endless repetition of pointless traditions, but the revival of the true freedom of every new generation who understands the power of the liberating Word of God.

The covenant is not words or stone tablets or legalistic correctness, but the joy and faith and life of a living people of God.

> 'I have given you as a covenant to the people,' says Isaiah, 'a light to the nations, to open the eyes that are blind, to bring out the prisoners from the dungeon, from the prison those who sit in darkness.' (42: 6, 7)

That is our mission in every new generation. It is not a threat to fear, but a proclamation to celebrate, a call to conversion, an invitation to a joyful responsibility, a hopeful enticement to learn to love again.

Not Moses, not Joshua, not our ancestors, but you, us, here, these ones, today, all of us, the living: *we* are called to claim the covenant and make it our own. To know the Lord, to do justice, to love mercy, and to walk humbly with our God.

Sometimes we come together and we speak nostalgically about the struggle against apartheid, of a time when the church was mightily involved, prophetically present, inspiring, courageous. We reminisce about those great moments: the marches we led, Bible in hand, falling on our knees as the casspirs arrived, praying while police pointed their guns and loosened their attack dogs. We speak of our church services and prayer meetings, preaching words of boldness and courage even while we knew the informers were in church, waiting to give taped copies of our sermons to their masters. We revel in the memory of how we faced the guns and the dogs, dragged the young people away from the tear gas and the sjamboks. We recall fondly how we comforted the children in prison and their shattered parents at home, telling them that the cause of justice calls for sacrifices and how, strengthened by our words, they rose, ready to once again make those sacrifices.

But times have changed, we tell ourselves now. Those days are gone forever. *That* struggle, *that* powerful creator of heroes, is over. *Our* challenges are different, so much more complex. Compassion for HIV/Aids victims versus budgetary constraints. Economic justice for the poor versus the demands of globalisation.

Land rights for the disinherited versus the expectations of foreign investors. The covenant we are speaking of, it was for *those* times, for *those* people, for another generation. I am here to tell you that the covenant stands, that it is meant for you, for us, living in South Africa today. The call for faithfulness, to do justice, to love mercy and to walk humbly with your God, it is for us, today, here, the living. The cries of the poor *today*, the pain of Aids victims *today*, the shattered dreams of so many *today*, all those are coming to us. We should stop reminiscing and respond to God's call to *us*, *today*. The covenant truly is meant for us. We should stop living in the past and be God's people *today*. God knows, as we do, that there is enough to for us to do.

But the times are evil, the church is but a small voice; believers get tired, preachers are not brave, nor angels. People get afraid, disappointments abound, the ministry is hard, the demands almost inhuman. What is left, is not us, or our strength, but the covenant, made not with others, but with us.

So then, you who are so directly spoken to by this God, you are no longer strangers and aliens, but you are citizens with the saints and also members of the family of God, built upon the foundation of the apostles and prophets, with Christ Jesus himself as the cornerstone. And he, Jesus, is the heart of the new covenant:

> His voice calls us,
> His death redeems us,
> His word emboldens us,
> His life inspires us,
> His Spirit empowers us,
> His resurrection revives us,
> His wounded hands heal us,
> He grace remakes us,
> His peace surrounds us,
> His presence overcomes us,
> His love sustains us.
> So his name be praised, today, now and for ever.

A Different Kind of War

After the death of Moses the servant of the LORD, the
LORD spoke to Joshua, son of Nun, Moses' assistant,
saying, 'My servant Moses is dead. Now proceed across
the Jordan, you and all this people, into the land that
I am giving to them, to the Israelites … As I was with
Moses, so I will be with you; I will not fail or forsake you.
Be strong and courageous; for you shall put this people
in possession of the land that I swore their ancestors to
give them. Only be very strong and courageous, being
careful to act in accordance with all the law that my
servant Moses commanded you; do not turn from it to
the right hand or the left, so that you may be successful
wherever you go. This book of the law shall not depart
out of your mouth; you shall meditate on it day and
night, so that you may be careful to act in accordance
with all that is written in it. For then you shall make
your way prosperous, and then you shall be successful.
I hereby command you, be strong and courageous; do
not be frightened or dismayed, for the LORD your
God is with you wherever you go … .' They answered
Joshua: 'All that you have commanded us we will do, and
wherever you send us we will go. Just as we obeyed
Moses in all things, so we will obey you. Only may the
LORD be with you, as he was with Moses! … Only be
strong and courageous.'

Joshua 1:1-9, 16-18

5

We have to be honest this morning. The book of Joshua is controversial. It leaves a sour taste in our mouths. It is a book about conquest and colonisation, of war and stolen land, subjection of peoples and the supremacy of military prowess, and all in the name of God.

For black Christians, as for all Christians with a sense of justice and compassion, Joshua is a hard pill to swallow. Those of us who have been colonised, subjected to the power of invaders or enslaved, do not find Joshua an easy book to read. After all, Hittites, Jebusites, Amorites and all the others lived there *first*. Peoples who have lost their land, have been taken as slaves, been colonised, subjected to strange masters, read these stories differently, if they read them at all. That long, depressing list of conquests should include our own, we know. And some of us avoid Joshua in our preaching schedule altogether, like the nineteenth-century black preacher in one of Professor James Cone's books who refused to preach 'from that fella Paul' because of Paul's perceived justification of slavery, used so well and effectively by the white preachers of the slave-holding South.

In modern Israel many, whose views are politically represented by the present Prime Minister Ariel Sharon (as are those of a generation of politicians before him), use Joshua as a basis for policies of land appropriation and oppression of the Palestinians, an interpretation of the book of Joshua which remains a strong element of the ongoing war and the elusive peace in the Middle East today. Likewise there are many, too many, right-wing fundamentalist Christians in the world, most of them in the United States of America, who share the same views, and have a disproportionate influence on American foreign policy as regards the Middle East. We, however, know that things, including history, are not that simple. From experience we know that not everything claimed to have been done in the name of the Bible is therefore correct. We are compelled to raise issues of justice; we are honour- bound to ask the question how, for instance, does a Palestinian Christian today read this book?

We, of course, do not have time to discuss all the issues this morning, but we do need to remember at least three things. First, the Bible itself is not at all unanimous in its telling of the 'conquest' of Canaan by Israel. Second, archeological research shows not a quick war of conquest but instead a gradual settlement of the tribes of Israel among the other peoples of the land. Inasmuch as there was fighting it seems plausible to suggest a rebellion of peasants against the ruling classes of the city-states, rather than an organizsed military invasion. Third, when read carefully, the whole book seems to be written more as *liturgical celebration* than as history. Joshua reflects Israel's faith rather than precise historical data regarding military actions.

That is not so strange. Much of what we call 'history' in the Bible is often not so much *what exactly happened,* as an attempt to ask: what is the message in the story? Africans are well acquainted with this. In the story of 'how the snake and the frog came to be enemies', the issue is not whether it actually happened exactly in that way, but rather, what does it tell us, what lessons do we learn from it? It is the same with, for example, Balaam's talking donkey in the book of Numbers, or with the story of Jonah. It will serve us well to remember the words of the great Swiss theologian Karl Barth, regarding the words of the snake in the garden of Eden. The issue, he said, is not whether the snake spoke; the question is rather *what did he say, and what does he say?*

But there is one more compelling reason why we should read this book differently. It *wants* to be read differently. Other books from the ancient Near East which claim to be history simply are not written in this way. It may be best to stipulate the issues, so that we can keep them clear in our own minds.

- Nowhere is there in the book of Joshua any sign of the glorification of military victories.
- In the theology of Israel *the land* is central. But the land is not *conquered land*, it is *promised* land. No less than six times in the first chapter we read of 'the land I have promised you' or 'the land I will give to you' (vv. 2, 3, 6, 11, 12, 15).

- Therefore the land is *given*. Land is life, and life is not a conquest; it is a *gift*. Land is space, sustenance, identity, sense of belonging. To have land is to have all this. To lose the land is to lose all this. But it is, and remains, a gift.
- There is very little emphasis on specific wars, and what details are given really stretch the imagination. Those wars are more miracle than good military strategy. The battle of Jericho is but one example.
- There are no heroes – at least not human ones. This is most unusual in historiography in ancient *and* modern times, for history evolves around the heroism of the leader, the general, the hero. This is true of the pharaohs of Egypt as it is of Alexander the Great, as it is of General Patton and General Louis Botha, Shaka of the Zulus, Norman Schwarzkopf and Colin Powell. In Joshua there is but *one* hero: Yahweh.

II

But if this is so, why then the repeated 'Be strong and full of courage', that seems to be the central motif of this passage? What does it mean?

Our book begins with the statement that Moses is dead. It is the end of an era; with Joshua, a new era begins. The people of Israel are standing on the banks of the river Jordan, just as they had once stood facing the Red Sea. There is some argument about this. For some this scene is a mere repetition of the Red Sea episode, more for effect than anything else. For others it is an attempt to legitimise Joshua as leader. Moses had his Red Sea to cross, Joshua must have his Jordan. For the people, this symbolism would have been powerful. It is as in modern politics: perception is everything.

I think this is beside the point. Jordan is a border, a moment in history. By crossing this river, Israel signifies that a new era has begun. A new life of challenges lies ahead, and this is but the first one. That's why the Hebrew emphatically says, '*this* Jordan' (v.2).

African-Americans, for example, understand this well. 'There is a river' has been a constant theme in African-American spirituality in the United States. It is also the title of a marvellous book with that theme by Vincent Harding. A river to cross, a mountain to climb, a new battle to fight. If you survive captivity and you go through that 'last door' on Goree Island, near Dakar in West Africa, to be herded onto a slave ship, that's a river to cross. On that ship, bracing yourself for the 'Middle Passage', that's one more river to cross. To survive that and be bought and sold like chattel, not knowing which was better: living or dying, that's a river to cross. To survive *that*, only to fight Jim Crow in the South and the more subtle, but nonetheless real racism of the North, is a river to cross. To reach deep inside yourself and to find, despite everything, the spiritual resources to wage a civil rights struggle that became a paradigm of the power of love versus loveless power: a river to cross. And now, still battling lingering, no, *festering* racism and our own complacency, we know we are standing before *this Jordan*, yet another river to cross.

Between these moments in history flows a river. It signifies a moment of pain and reflection, as well as a moment of decision. This is why the Bible pauses at 'this Jordan'. Israel's life is irrevocably changing. It is leaving the wilderness behind where it dwelt in virtual isolation, moving into a settled and organised land. The question the river poses is: what will happen now?

What will Israel's life be in the midst of these other peoples with their religions, their gods and temples, their beliefs and stories, their advanced cultures and sciences? What will Israel do with its one, invisible God, a concept that was unique, utterly unheard of and laughably foolish: a god one cannot see, who lives not in a temple but in a tent, not represented by a golden statue but by a wooden box holding two stone tablets? A God without these grandiose, outward signs of power?

How will Israel remain faithful, remain *people of God*? How will they keep their faith – with the power of the weapons of war through which others will be subjugated and forced on their knees before this God, or with the power of the Word of God in their hearts and on their lips?

These are the questions Israel faces as the people stand on the banks of that river, looking upon a land they have never before seen, peoples they do not understand, a future they could not know.

III

In light of this, I believe that the oft-repeated words 'be strong and full of courage' are not encouragement for military confrontation, but encouragement for a different kind of war: the struggle for faithfulness in a new land, amongst other peoples. Here, their faith will be tested, not by hunger or thirst, but by other challenges: why do you believe what you believe? Why are you so different? Who is this God whom you worship? No, these words do not refer to preparedness for war. They refer to the witness of Israel, to the challenge of obedience, to faithfulness. If we read well, we will perceive this almost immediately. Nowhere are these words linked to preparedness for war. Already in vv. 6 and 7 the words 'Be strong and courageous' belong inextricably to the admonition to 'being careful to act in accordance with all the law that my servant Moses commanded you …'. It is not military power that would make the people successful, but their obedient ability 'not to turn from [The law] to the right hand or the left.' It is not military strength that shall make Joshua prosperous, but the book of the law, if it does 'not depart out of your mouth'. The fight is not for military superiority; it is for prophetic faithfulness.

In some small way, we know that to be true. How natural is it for us to testify to our faith outside the walls of the church, in the circle of our intellectual friends who think faith is a joke, or at the very least a crutch for the intellectually deprived, for those who cannot face life on its own terms? How hard is it for us to trust God wholeheartedly when to keep as tight a control of our lives as possible is our dearest wish? How hard is it to live by faith when it is taunted by the logic by which we exist? What does it mean to be a church when it makes so little difference to so many? How faithful and strong and courageous are we then?

For these reasons I believe that the most important words, the leitmotif of our text, are not the words we read in vv. 6, 7, 9 and 18:

'Be strong and full of courage …'. I think the key to this text is in verse 17, the fervent prayer of the people as they address Joshua: 'Only, may the LORD be with you as He was with Moses.' For this, then and now, is the secret. Not power or might or cleverness, but the nearness of God.

IV

The times are changing. We are three years into the new millennium. We are standing on the banks of another river, we are crossing 'this' Jordan. The last fifty years of the last century have for ever changed our world, the way we live, the way we believe. The 'war to end all wars' has produced more wars than we care to count. Our technological progress has brought us face to face with the ultimate temptation: not just to *play* God (we have been doing that for as long as anyone can remember), but to *replace* God. Our ability to serve life has proved to be astonishing; our ability to destroy life has become horrific. Even as we touch the gates of heaven, we are shackled to the portals of hell.

The Christian church here, and elsewhere, is no longer the strong voice of a strong nation. And that is good. The church should not reflect the 'strength' of the nation, nor should we depend on it. We can no longer speak if we do not also listen to the voice of other communities of faith. We are told that Islam is now the fastest growing faith in the United States, and in South Africa it is growing too. There are some who are disturbed by this. But what should really disturb us is that it is also clear that Muslims are far more serious about their faith than 'mainline' Christians are about theirs. There are those of us who long for the days when the church in South Africa spoke clearly, prophetically, inspirationally to the powers that be as well as to the people. But the voice of the church was heard, not because it was connected to power but because it spoke *truth*. And if we depend upon God's truth rather than on worldly power, we may yet rediscover the power of the church.

Moreover, we know ourselves better. We know what has been done in the name of God; that the church has too often justified violence and war, death and destruction. We have too often denounced life, denied others, betrayed our Lord. The greatest struggles have always been against slavery *and* the Bible, racism *and* the Bible, apartheid *and* the Bible, misogyny *and* the Bible, violence and the Bible. Even now, what we know as 'Christian' politics in America for instance, means justification of racism, sanctification of war, the enslavement of women, marginalisation of the poor, demonisation of lesbians and gays. And it is with dismay that we see *that* brand of Christianity also growing in South Africa. I know that there are millions of 'fundamentalist Muslims' who use the Qur'an to justify war, violence, oppression and terrorism. But they are not the issue this morning. We are.

We continue to face the same questions: what do you believe? Why do you believe? Who is your God? Do you know who *you* are? How will we remain faithful? In other words, are we ready for this war? Oh, I know, America is ready. It is already the number one military nation in the world. But is it ready to fight poverty, racism and bigotry? I know South Africa is ready. It is, and has been since the apartheid days, the strongest country economically on the continent, with the best equipped army, with our own weapons industry. But is it ready to do justice to the poor, to set an example in the fair distribution of land, to resist the temptation of tribalism which is already plaguing us in ways we would deny rather than fight?

It seems to me I can do no better than to offer the prayer the people offered for Joshua: May the LORD be with you as he was with Moses. And I offer this prayer to our people *and* our leaders, for this is what we mean when we say our 'Prayer for Africa': 'God bless Africa, guide her leaders, give her peace.' We pray that God will be with us as the LORD was with Moses at the burning bush, making him stand on holy ground. Since that moment Israel always knew it to be thus: when we are in the presence of God, we are on holy ground. We need to think about that. Why are our churches dying, our prayers too much like sand between our teeth, our theology dry as dust, our worship as wind and our sermons often not a word from the Lord but blasphemous, if pious, prattle? We have forgotten that we are standing on holy ground.

May the LORD be with you like he was with Moses, when he told the Pharaoh: 'Let my people go!' It needs still to be heard, in a time when oppression takes on more subtle, and therefore more deadly forms; when poverty is growing and destitution and fear for the future drive senior citizens to suicide, because for them, 'welfare reform' means death. It needs to be heard in a time when black Americans can be enlisted on the side of the racists, bought to defile Martin King's memory by using his sacrifice to paralyse the struggle against racism.

May the LORD be with you, as God was with Moses, as he stood before his people, not afraid to tell them the truth: 'You perverse and crooked generation! Do you thus repay the LORD? Is He not your Father, who created you, who made and established you – remember the days of old!' It needs to be heard, that prophetic voice, in a time when violence is tearing our communities apart and the new rap culture becomes as effective an assault on our dignity as slavery and apartheid were. It needs to be heard, in the face of so much complacency, when many of us are so blind with joy to be part of a new, wealthy elite that we no longer see the wretchedness of so many around us.

How are we to be a church in an age where the forces of evil will be more powerful than ever, and more invisible than ever? To see what most refuse to see? To hear the cries of the silenced? To speak out where others are too afraid? That's a different kind of war. To speak truth to power, to seek to be faithful rather than popular; to resist unjust policies even as they parade as Christian virtues; to stand by the poor, the hurt, the rejected, the excluded in a society that is designed to make them invisible – that's a different kind of war.

We cannot do without this prayer. May the LORD be with you, as he was with Moses. And as we prepare ourselves for this different kind of battle, let us prayerfully remember:

If the LORD is with us, we will be faithful;

if the LORD is with us, we will do what is right, not because we will succeed, but because *it is right*;

if the LORD is with us, our faith will be the rock upon which he will build his church, and the gates of hell shall not prevail against it.

If the LORD is with us, we will renew our strength, we will mount up like eagles, we will run and not grow weary, we shall walk and not faint.

If the LORD is with us, every valley shall be lifted and every mountain and hill made low; the crooked places shall be made straight and the rough places plain.

Then the glory of the LORD shall be revealed, and all flesh shall see it together.

The Tears of the Sower

When the LORD restored the
fortunes of Zion,
we were like those who dream.
Then our mouth was filled with
laughter,
And our tongue with shouts of joy;
then it was said among the nations,
'The LORD has done great
things for them.'
The LORD has done great things for us,
and we rejoiced.
Restore our fortunes, O LORD,
like the watercourses in the Negeb.
May those who sow in tears
reap with shouts of joy.
Those who go out weeping,
bearing the seed for sowing,
shall come home with shouts of joy,
carrying their sheaves.

Psalm 126

6

Psalm 126 is a riddle, a perplexity, really. A sower who weeps, is that not an impossibility? Isn't it as incongruous as an undertaker cracking jokes at the graveside? After all, to be sowing again, what a wondrous, joyful thing! You have land, it has not been stolen, or claimed in debt, or estranged from your family for some reason. There is no threat; clouds of war do not darken the sky, there is no enemy at the gates. The previous harvest was rich enough to have left you with seed to sow, it has rained, the land is ready, and there is yet another harvest to look forward to.

So why does the sower weep? In an agrarian society the very act of sowing is a sign of prosperity and peace, a testimony of hope. The joy of sowing is surpassed only by the joy of the harvest. So the psalm presents us with a puzzle: this sower who stands in his field like a weeping willow.

But then the whole psalm is a vortex of clashing emotions. The first part is a hymn of praise, the second part is a sorrow song. Verse 2 speaks of laughing, verse 3 of rejoicing, vv. 5 and 6 of tears and weeping. There is a strange mixture of pain and joy, of hope and desperation. In fact Psalm 126, as a whole, is framed in painful contradiction.

Verse 1 rejoices: 'When the LORD restored the fortunes of Zion, we were like those who dream … .' Verse 4 cries out: 'Restore our fortunes, O LORD!' As if nothing had happened. As if verse 1 was a mistake that should now be rectified. How is that possible? Their fortunes *have* been restored, have they not? The LORD *has* done great things, has He not? Why cry out in longing for something you already have? The problem is so perplexing that some scholars are arguing for two separate psalms, with two separate themes, written in different times, only later joined by one editor. But that seems to me to be a solution a bit too extreme. Let us take some time and wrestle a bit with this intriguing portion of Scripture.

II

Psalm 126 was written after the exile. The people have returned, Jerusalem is being rebuilt, the temple is arising slowly and Israel is becoming Israel again. The wounds are beginning to heal now. They are restoring their homes, they are sowing in their own fields again. What they thought would not be possible, has actually happened: Yahweh has heard their cries, their redemption has come, their exile is over. What they had heard the prophets say was no dream:

> The nations shall see your vindication and all the kings
> your glory; ... You shall no more be termed Forsaken,
> and your land shall no more be called Desolate ...
> The LORD has sworn by his right hand ... I will not
> again give you grain to be food for your enemies, and
> foreigners shall not drink the wine for which you have
> laboured ... . (Isaiah 62: 2, 4, 8)

The word of the LORD was not spoken in vain and the faithfulness of Yahweh is there for all to see. And they know it too: 'The LORD has done great things for us!' They rejoiced.

But note something strange: Israel confesses this only after others have said it. The greatness of God toward Israel is exclaimed first by 'the nations'. Israel has to be *reminded*. Is Israel already so jaded, so blasé, that the great deeds of God's liberation are taken for granted, or within the greater historical scheme of things, not noticed? Or are they so ungrateful that they accept all this as their *due*, as if God had no choice but to help them, as if God was obligated? Why does verse 3 sound like an afterthought, and why does their 'rejoicing' have the sound of a belated, if not a reluctant, celebration? It seems an acknowledgement of God's greatness only grudgingly given: since even the heathen recognise Israel's liberation as a 'great thing' done by the LORD. Israel has no choice but to agree. Is this what we are facing here: God, the great burden of the chosen? Or, is this, perhaps, a repeat of the shameless, thankless bickering Moses had to contend with and which so exasperated Yahweh?

> … Was it because there were no graves in Egypt that
> you have taken us away to die in the wilderness? What
> have you done to us, bringing us out of Egypt?
> (Exodus 14:11)

All these questions are valid, and all of the above might even be true. After all, Israel is not so different from us: our taking God's great deeds for granted, acting as if we deserved them; our embarrassment in acknowledging that it is *God* who acts for our sake, until those outside the church voice their surprise that we do not see it. And it is true: the LORD *has* done great things for us, only in the new South Africa we are so bent on denying that, that God has all but disappeared from the struggle and the heartbeat of our new democracy. In ten years of democracy, we have truly come a long way. But we speak and act as if everything we have been able to achieve has been the fruit of our own ingenuity, our political astuteness, our clever compromises. They speak of a 'miracle', our politicians, our academics and our media, but the source of that miracle they find within ourselves. But Christians know better. Yet, if we knew better, why are we so silent? Why are we so tongue-tied about what we believed and knew to be true throughout the struggle: that 'if it were not for the LORD, *let Israel say it! ...*'. Through our silence, we allow God to be robbed of his glory and we are bereft of joy. So it might indeed be true.

But I think there is something else here. The tears of the sower are neither tears of petulance nor ingratitude. The cry of verse 4 is voiced not out of anger or cynicism, but out of genuine distress and perplexity. Israel wrestles not with her ungrateful heart, but with the complexity and incomprehensibility of life. The exile is over, but liberation has not yet come. That is the crux of the matter, and that is why the sower weeps. The 'liberation' has been hijacked by the powerful, and given a meaning that excludes the powerless. For many in Israel, the return to their land does not fulfil the need for a happy, meaningful life.

Exile has ended, but in Jerusalem and the far-flung areas in the land, for the poor, the weak and the needy it makes no difference whatsoever. It is this situation that is so powerfully captured by

Habakkuk: the people have returned, the state is restored, the temple is rebuilt, but justice hangs in the willows like a discarded, unplayed harp:

> O LORD, how long shall I cry for help, and you will not listen? … Destruction and violence are before me; strife and contention arise. So the law becomes slack and justice never prevails. The wicked surround the righteous – therefore judgement comes forth perverted. (1: 2-4)

No sooner have they returned that Isaiah has this to say:

> All you wild animals, all you wild animals in the forest, come to devour! Israel's sentinels are blind, they are all without knowledge … They are like dogs … [with] a mighty appetite; they never have enough. The shepherds also have no understanding; they have all turned to their own way, to their own gain one and all. (56: 9-11)

It seems that Israel had not learned a single lesson in exile. They have carried with them into exile, and they have brought back with them from exile the very things that have caused their downfall and their loss: greed, rapaciousness, injustice, exploitation and a lack of compassion. The word of the LORD was clear:

> Act with justice and righteousness, and deliver from the hand of the oppressor anyone who has been robbed. And do no wrong or violence to the alien, the orphan, and the widow, or shed innocent blood in this place. (Jeremiah 22: 3)

They did not listen then, and obedience seems equally hard for them now. They return, the powerful to their seats of power, the powerless to their misery. Even the shared pain and the solidarity of exile could not demolish the divisions of class and privilege. The injustices of the past flourish easier than the newly planted wheat and the walls between the rich and the poor are rebuilt faster than the walls of the temple.

III

There are some who say that the poor, the women, the downtrodden, should not look to the Bible for comfort. The Bible, they argue, is much too much a book written by the scribes and secretaries of kings and men of power; by learned priests who represented only the interests of the ruling classes. It is a book filled with what they call 'royal theology', a theology sensitive only to the needs of the rich and the powerful. I do not totally agree with them although in all honesty they have a point. There are portions of the Bible that emanate from the palaces and the rooms of royal scribes, but this is not the place to pursue that particular argument. It is clear to me, however, despite the presence of the 'royal theology', that the reality which gave birth to the psalms in general, and Psalm 126 in particular, was not within the gilded walls of the new palaces but in the wide open spaces of the fields. Not by well-fed priests in the service of the rich, but by weeping peasants with a bag of precious seed slung over their shoulders.

They, the poor and the needy, have discovered what the poor have known ever since, and it is this: no matter how romantic the revolution, no matter how persuasive the slogans, liberation is incremental, and they are not the first. They are the revolution's afterthought. That is why Israel's song so quickly becomes a moan: 'Restore our fortunes, O LORD.' That is the misery that accompanies all human liberation. We struggle for freedom, for the restoration of our human rights, for dignity and justice, and so we must. But almost always our struggle turns upon us, our new-found freedom becomes an iron cage, and the revolution disclaims, disinherits, and dishonours its children. The goals we fought for remain elusive dreams, and our disappointment is as acrid as the smoke that hangs over our burnt-out hopes.

When the Berlin Wall fell in 1989, the events reverberated around the world. A stunned humanity watched as, brick by brick, the symbol of one of modern history's most awesome and powerful ideologies was broken down. Communism, and all the awe-inspiring symbolism that went with it, was officially over, and having become victim to the fury of the very masses upon whom it preyed, soon had to struggle to survive. For many in Eastern Europe, it was like a dream.

And then came Bosnia, Herzegovina, Serbia, and later Kosovo; wars that stunned the world by their ferocity and brutality. And the lethargy of the rest of Europe was the most eloquent testimony of the folly of human arrogance. They were so cocksure that such a thing was impossible in Europe, that they were totally unprepared for it. Meanwhile, the world was forced to add two new words to our vocabulary of horror: 'ethnic cleansing'. Too soon the dream shattered, and the hopes for democracy and freedom drowned in rivers of blood.

Restore our fortunes, O LORD!

In South Africa apartheid is over, but apartheid is everywhere. The oppressors of yesterday live as well as ever; the murderers of our children and the artists of the torture chambers walk the streets as cocky as ever. The power relationships have hardly shifted, and the grip of the old, white, moneyed establishment on almost every facet of life is fearsome. Racism, even though vehemently denied, continues to plague us, and fathers bitter injustice in our courts. HIV/Aids is a raging beast that is seeking to destroy the future of our nation, and our politicians play word games. The gap between the new black elite and the poor black masses is as wide as any gap that ever existed, only more pain-filled. And in the impoverished rural areas and the teeming squatter camps, where the pain was always greatest, they still hear that they must 'tighten their belts' while parliamentarians voted in by the loyalty and hopes of the poor, vote themselves two salary increases in one year.

We thought we were free; we thought exile was over. Twenty years ago, in a sermon that caused some anger in establishment circles and earned me a grave warning from a cabinet minister, I quoted a passage from Shakespeare's *Macbeth* that caught the mood perfectly. I can still quote it now, even though the irony hurts more than I can say:

Alas, poor country,
almost afraid to know itself!
It cannot be call'd our mother,
but our grave.
Where nothing, but who knows nothing
is once seen to smile;
Where sighs and groans and shrieks
that rend the air
are made, not marked; where sorrow
seems a modern ecstasy.

For still the voices of the poor are unheard, and when the Archbishop of Cape Town dares to speak on their behalf he is cut down by the new president as efficiently as was done by the P W Bothas of old. Even in this regard, so very little has changed. The church in South Africa, if it once again wants to be prophetic, has painful choices to make.

We *thought* we were free.

Restore our fortunes, O LORD!

And what of the United States where people are made to believe that they were solely responsible for the fall of communism? Where the idols of capitalism and 'market democracy' reign with even greater arrogance since they have outlived communism and hence think they will live for ever? Here the gap between rich and poor is larger than in any industrialised country in the world. The disparities are as staggering as they are disturbing: one half of one per cent owns thirty-three per cent of the total wealth in this country; nine-and-a-half per cent owns thirty-six per cent and the rest (ninety per cent) share the thirty per cent that's left.

In the United States, what experts call 'real hunger' has become a common phenomenon. 'Welfare reform' hit the poor, the needy and the elderly, but subsidies for wealthy large companies are growing. It is not just that racism is proliferating, for it has never really died; it is the respectability in which it is cloaked and the vehemence with which it is being denied by so many that I find truly frightening.

More than thirty years ago the words 'Let freedom ring' echoed from the Lincoln Memorial and helped shape a dream that inspired millions across the world who were struggling for their freedom. They warmed our hearts and we all dreamt the dream of justice, peace, love and racial harmony. Today, amidst the growing darkness of racial mistrust and alienation, we hardly know what that means anymore.

Restore our fortunes, O LORD!

That is the epilogue of human liberation: sowing with tears, the new beginning that dies before it has had a chance to live. We had better face it: we need more than political liberation, more than the freedom promised by easy slogans, more than the 'better life' we will have after we have given our vote away. We need more than laws that can be rewritten so easily thirty years later. We need more than the slick, anaesthetic propaganda spouted on television and radio, dished up in media owned by the few rich who know nothing of the realities of pain and struggle.

We need a deeper commitment to justice and to each other. We need a deeper commitment to God. We need Someone whose Word remains for ever, whose love is everlasting, whose mercy is greater than our ability to succeed or fail, in whom we can truly put our trust. We need Someone who can bring wholeness to our shattered existence, in whom our struggles for justice and liberation can be anchored. We need to know a freedom that is greater than the freedom promised by political programmes and party platforms. We need an obedience that transcends party loyalty and the need for political compromise. Let's be honest: we need Jesus.

IV

The sower goes out weeping, sowing in tears, vv. 5 and 6 tell us. The repetition emphasises the mood. Again, why? There is, I think, a second reason. The sower weeps, for he has so little. Palestinian farmers were poor, their land, if they owned it at all, was small. Rainfall was scarce, and certainly not guaranteed. Unlike the rich landowner, they did not have storage rooms stacked to the ceilings.

The surplus from the previous harvest might have been enough, but never abundant. What they had, therefore, was in reality not much at all.

The seed he sows is *grain*. It could have been ground into flour to make bread for his family. It is *bread* he is putting into the ground. What guarantee is there that it will grow? Or of rain, or of a year free of calamity? So, painful choices must be made here. He must open his hand and let go of what he has, in hopes of something he cannot guarantee or control. He must let go of the certainty of today for the hope of tomorrow. He must let go in the faith that this seed, too, will become grain, food for his children.

That is more than a cautious, close-fisted Calvinist can bear, I should think. Can we do it? Open our hands to give up our certainties for the faith that God will do as God has promised? Sow the seed – however little it is we have – in the faith that God will give grain? Can we give up the faith in shaky political programmes and ideological convictions and place our faith in something at once more unseen and yet more certain? Can we work and sow, through tears if necessary, knowing that we will reap the harvest with joy? Can we shed tears of anguish for the injustices ravaging our world and still continue to work for justice?

Can we continue to do what is right, to fight for justice, to seek the things that make for peace, even as we know that human greed, avarice and rapaciousness will seek to thwart our efforts? Can we do it, not because we know we will succeed, but because it is right in God's sight? You see, the sower weeps, but he is not condemned. But neither is he deterred. Even as he weeps he sows, in the firm faith that he shall come back with shouts of joy, carrying the sheaves. He weeps, *but he does not stop sowing*. His tears for the hardness of human sinfulness and the stubborn unwillingness to do God's will do not deny him the joy of his faith in the God whose promises are never broken. Can we do it? Working for justice even as we long for the fulfilment of God's Kingdom? Can the longing for the unseen Kingdom sustain us through and beyond the realities of struggle? Can we walk by faith, and not by sight?

CHAPTER 6

Because that is what God does with us. *'For God so loved the world, that He gave his only begotten Son, that whosoever believes in him, should not perish, but have everlasting life'* (John 3:16). We know this text so well, we hardly think about the devastating truth that it reveals. God gave God's son, but there was no guarantee that we would believe, or love in return. God just did it. There was no effort to first exact promises from us, there was no manoeuvring for some fall-back position. God just did it.

It is actually quite breathtaking when we stop to think about it.

Jesus is the opened hands of God, the silent prayer on the lips of God, the burning hope in the heart of God: if my people, whom I have called by my name, see this, they too, will love and believe. But, and this is the amazing thing, God can only hope. There is no guarantee. And so Psalm 126 places us before yet another perplexity. And this perplexity of divine love and mercy is greater than the incomprehensibility of life we discovered in the psalm: it enfolds it, overcomes it, breaks it open.

The puzzle of the psalmist still exists, but it is no longer devastating. We know now why the sower is weeping. We know, too, that the weeping will last 'only for a night, for joy comes in the morning'. We know too, that we, even though we sow in tears, will come home carrying the sheaves with joy. The NRSV translation, *'May* those who sow in tears reap with sounds of joy' is tinged with a postmodern tentativeness that is completely absent in the exuberant certainty of the Hebrew. There the affirmation is much stronger: 'Those who sow in tears *shall* reap with shouts of joy.' The psalmist is rejoicing in the unseen, the hoped for, the not yet accomplished. Human hardness is challenged by the love of God. Human unwillingness is subverted by the generosity of God. Human resistance is overcome by the unrestrained commitment of God. Human freedom is guaranteed by the freedom of the Living One who chose to become less than God for our sake. Human justice is grounded in the justice of the God of Israel who delivered Israel from Egypt and from Babylon. The untrustworthiness of the revolution is subject to the compassionate justice and everlasting love of the Living God.

Therefore, my beloved, be steadfast, immovable, always excelling in the work of the Lord, because you know that in the Lord your labour is not in vain.

(1 Corinthians 15:58)

A Name Better than Children

Thus says the LORD: Maintain justice, and do what
is right, for soon my salvation will come, and my
deliverance be revealed. Happy is the mortal who does
this, the one who holds it fast, who keeps the Sabbath,
not profaning it, and refrains from doing any evil. Do not
let the foreigner joined to the LORD say, 'The LORD
will surely separate me from his people'; and do not let
the eunuch say, 'I am just a dry tree'. For thus says the
LORD: To the eunuchs who keep my Sabbaths, who
choose the things that please me and hold fast my
covenant, I will give, in my house and within my walls, a
monument and a name better than sons and daughters;
I will give them an everlasting name that shall not be
cut off. And the foreigners who join themselves to the
LORD, to minister to him, to love the name of the
LORD, and to be his servants, all who keep the Sabbath,
and do not profane it, and hold fast my covenant
– these I will bring to my holy mountain, and make
them joyful in my house of prayer; their burnt offerings
and their sacrifices will be accepted on my altar; for my
house shall be called a house of prayer for all peoples.
Thus says the LORD God, who gathers the outcasts of
Israel, I will gather others to them besides those already
gathered.

Isaiah 56:1-8

Today we are burying Douglas Hevenor. He finally lost his battle against the disease that has ravaged his body for so long.

What do we know about Doug?

That he was a kind, gentle man, an artist of no mean reputation, a gifted dancer who danced with the likes of Margot Fonteyn. A good friend, full of fun and humour – the evidence of which we have heard all through this service.

But we know more. Douglas Hevenor was a gay man. And one who did not try to hide it. He had no wife, no children. No name to leave behind. His line ends here.

For many in this country and elsewhere his lifestyle was an unspeakable sin in God's eyes. For them, he was despicable in life, and in death he is doomed. Said one famous televangelist just the other day: 'Because of [people like him] America's name shall be wiped off the face of the earth', just as, presumably, Doug's name should be wiped off the face of the earth. His very existence is an affront to a 'Christian' country, to Christian people everywhere. So he should not be remembered, there should be no monuments of any kind. His *life* ends here.

The sooner he is forgotten, the better it will be.

II

No! says God. 'I will give, in my house and within my walls, a monument and a name better than sons and daughters; I will give them an everlasting name that shall not be cut off.'

This comes in the middle of one of the most beloved portions of the Hebrew Bible – 'the book of consolation', second Isaiah. For Israel, in exile, lost, dislocated and disheartened, this is where the tide turns. Gone, for the moment, are the castigations, the reminders of their sinfulness which caused a wall between themselves and their God. Silent too, is the voice of reproach, which spoke of a rebellious, faithless people, 'who carry out a plan, but not mine' (Isaiah 30:1), who honour 'me with their lips' while their hearts are 'far from me', the One whom Israel has 'deeply betrayed'.

Israel's fortunes are about to be restored, its restoration is about to commence. So, instead of condemnation, they hear words of comfort; instead of being disowned, Israel is claimed; instead of having no name, Israel is called by name: 'Jacob, my chosen', 'offspring of Abraham, my friend', 'Israel, in whom I will be glorified'. Instead of being dispersed, Israel is gathered. Instead of being rejected, Israel is honoured.

These words are like a fresh breeze on a glowing face, cool water on a parched tongue.

In exile, Israelites felt themselves forgotten, rejected, scattered, oppressed, discarded; but most of all, excluded from the presence of Yahweh, cut off from the Covenant, languishing in the darkness, outside of the wideness of God's mercy.

Isaiah 40 to 66 is God's announcement that that is all over; it is all being overturned. For that reason the words 'gathered', 'accepted', 'not cut off', 'covenant', and 'hold fast' are so special, so poignant, so pregnant with meaning, so heavy with redemption. Isaiah expressly uses them in counterpoint to the words used before. And the contrast is striking, joyously liberating.

But here is the first surprise. The great thing about the restoration of Israel in second Isaiah is not so much the rebuilding of the walls of Jerusalem or the temple. It is not so much the rediscovery of their national identity, nor the re-establishment of the throne of David – however important these may have been to many in Israel. The thing is that Israel understands, finally, what it means to be the people of God. Hence the prophet's choice of words like 'gathered' and 'accepted' and 'chosen'.

At first the tone is generous, wide, sweeping. It is all about Israel, Jacob, the people, the nation. Like full, orchestral, symphonic waves, the music Isaiah composes is grand, majestic. From chapter 40:

> Comfort, o comfort my people, says your God. Speak
> tenderly to Jerusalem, and cry to her that she has
> served her term, that her penalty is paid ... .

From chapter 42:

> Here is my servant, whom I uphold, my chosen, in
> whom my soul delights ... .

From chapter 49, more tender still:

> See, I have inscribed you in the palm of my hand ... .

In chapter 50, Israel is told what it means when the LORD is on her side, and the rebuke is more out of frustrated love than out of anger:

> Why was no one there when I came? Why did no one
> answer when I called? Is my hand shortened, that it
> cannot redeem? Or have I no power to deliver?

Israel now responds with the confidence of one who is taught by the LORD:

> The LORD God helps me; ... I know I shall not be put
> to shame ... Who will contend with me?

In chapter 51, the call is upon the LORD:

> Awake, awake, put on strength, O arm of the LORD!

But by chapter 52 the startling call is made on Israel herself:

> Awake, awake, put on your strength, O Zion! ...
> Depart, depart, go out from there!

And then the unforgettable:

> How beautiful upon the mountains are the feet of the
> messenger who announces peace ... who says to Zion:
> 'Your God reigns!'

III

But then the mood changes. Suddenly the orchestra is silent. Out of nowhere comes the sound of the oboe, a single note, suspended on a breath of pure sweetness. It begins in chapter 54:1:

> Sing, o barren one who did not bear … do not fear,
> for you will not be ashamed … For your maker is your
> husband, the LORD of hosts is his name, the Holy One
> of Israel is your redeemer … .

Some exegetes see this one barren woman as a continued symbol of the people of Israel. I disagree. The spotlight now is not on the people as a whole, but on this one person with all her pain, her suffering, her longing. The voice is not the amplified tones of one addressing the masses, but the gentle whisper into a single ear. She is singled out; she stands for those in the community who have suffered even more than just the suffering of exile. She symbolises those whose particular pain has been snowed under the collective pain of the people as a whole. Those whose personal pain had to remain unnoticed, unmentioned and unmourned because of the overwhelming vastness of the collective misery.

Yet it is the very stillness of this voice, the quiet concentration on this one soul that focuses our attention. It is not possible to miss her:

> For a brief moment I abandoned you, but with great
> compassion I will gather you. In overflowing wrath for
> a moment I hid my face from you, but with everlasting
> love I will have compassion on you … .

Neither is it possible to miss the pain of regret in the voice of God. That poignant 'for a moment', *twice*, is contrite, almost an apology. Can you imagine that? We are stunned by the depth of mercy, by the humility of holiness. Yahweh is shattered: 'Have I been too harsh?' God makes up in double measure: that 'brief' moment must surely be overshadowed, and eliminated, God hopes, by the 'everlasting' love and compassion. The time in exile does not weigh up to the steadfastness of God's love.

It is not by accident that the theme of childlessness is introduced. It calls to mind those fragile, foundational moments in Israel's history when Israel collectively held its breath: with Sarah, and Rebecca, Rachel and Hannah. The issue goes beyond the strength of the tribe, financial insecurity and lack of guarantees for old age. It highlights a real and terrible pain in Israel, and reveals within itself all the horrors of exile: the suffering, the insecurity, the rejection, and above all, the feeling of being excluded.

As a people, Israel's suffering in exile is real, but it is time now to reveal the pain within the pain. The oboe is joined by the strings, and the woman is joined by others so much like her. 'Do not let the foreigner say ... do not let the eunuch say ... .' The rhythm is strong, the theme is compelling. Those who do not have this pain must share it and take it away, for that is what it means to 'maintain justice and do what is right' with which portentous words this portion begins. (56:1)

> For thus says the LORD: To the eunuchs, I will give ...
> and the foreigners I will bring ... .

The end of the exile of the people *must* mean the end of the pain of the outcast. Without this, the end of the exile is meaningless. Yahweh is adamant: the collective pain, however intense, cannot serve as easy cover for the personal pain. The oppression caused by the enemy without cannot and shall not camouflage the suffering and oppression caused by Israel's heartlessness towards its own. For Israel to 'rejoice' in her return, these outcasts must 'be joyful in my house of prayer'. And the prophet mentions them by name.

IV

God speaks, not to 'the people' in general, but to those who have always been despised, rejected, looked down upon, excluded: women, childless women (for it was always the fault of the women), foreigners, eunuchs. Not for nothing is the word 'outcasts' used so repeatedly and emphatically.

We, Christians at the end of the second millennium after Christ, and even farther removed from Isaiah, are so blinded by prejudice, so jaded by bigotry, so blunted by hypocrisy that we have no idea how disturbing, how utterly revolutionary that must have sounded. The reality of exile brings a common sense of oppression, of collective suffering, of communal struggle, of a shared longing for freedom and restoration. Amongst that multitude of voices, no single voice is allowed to be heard; it is a distraction, an unwanted call for individual attention. It is unacceptable, almost obscene, certainly an affront, to introduce the pain of individual groups within the community. No one, in *that situation*, wants to be reminded of oppression *within* when all the attention should be on the oppression from without.

I think I can understand that well. It was exactly the same in the struggle against apartheid. What counted was the common struggle against white racism, economic exploitation and political oppression. Few would dare raise questions of oppression internal to the struggle. Few would dare to 'confuse' the issue by raising questions about the insensitivity of the liberation movement to myriad issues pertaining to groups who felt themselves locked out, sat upon, disregarded, even as they marched and suffered with the rest of us. They were expected to subject their own, real pain to the greater suffering of 'the masses'. Gays knew it; women knew it, dissidents knew it, and so too those whose human rights were trampled underfoot in the military camps in the bush. We needed to remain focussed. We needed to remain together. And our togetherness could not abide attention to the terrible aloneness of an individual, caused by us. At the funerals of those who were murdered by the police or the soldiers the cry was, 'Don't mourn, mobilise!' Mourning was a sign of weakness: the regime has won. They should not be allowed to see it, lest they rejoice in it. The grief of loved ones had to be a very private grief, so that the rhythm of struggle would not be disturbed.

So no one speaks out. But Isaiah does. Because God cares. And here is the difference between prophecy and demagoguery.

And so we are forced to look at this childless woman who shall not disappear into the vast, oppressed masses. Not to have a child in Israel was to have no name, no hope, no future. It was to be outside the circle, cut off from the covenant, excluded from the promises of

Yahweh to Abraham. You did not really belong to the chosen, you were not *gathered* by the LORD.

Barren women, foreigners who were not children of Abraham, and eunuchs, men who could not have children, were the personification of all those excluded from God's grace. Outcasts, Isaiah calls them.

This was true for castrated men (Leviticus 23:1), as it was for men whose manhood was considered impaired. It is all these, says John Calvin in his commentary on Isaiah, the despised and rejected, excluded from the promises of God to Abraham, whom the prophet has in mind. If modern commentaries, following Calvin's lead, include women, the poor, the needy, and the despised, who are not mentioned here, and they do, then we must include those whom Isaiah does mention. And the message comes to all, gay men and lesbian women, as well as the childless, the unmarried, the unchosen, the unpartnered.

What Isaiah is saying is this: Israel, your comfort is naught if it is not comfort for the least considered and the most despised. Your restoration is vain if it is not *their* restoration. Your identity no longer lies in their exclusion, but rather you shall be known by your inclusiveness. Your wholeness lies in the celebration of their joyful presence in your midst and in the house of the LORD. And the criteria for this acceptance and affirmation are not the moral and political vagaries of fickle human beings, not the smaller or greater hypocrisies with which we try to out-moralise God, but criteria set by Yahweh for *all* who love the LORD: 'If they choose the things that please me … if they hold fast my covenant … If they keep my Sabbaths …'. Exactly what Yahweh demands from all of us. These are God's chosen ones. They do not have to please *us*, they must please the LORD. No wonder God instructs Isaiah to begin with 'Maintain justice …'.

V

This is stunning, truly amazing. And only now does the whole orchestra join in, and the majesty of it, the grandness of it, sweeps us away:

> Thus says the LORD, who gathers the outcasts of Israel
> – I will gather them besides those already gathered.

In other words, their gathering is a separate act of God. Is it because God knows that out of itself Israel will not consider them 'gathered', does not want them gathered? If this is so, and I think it is, then this act of God is simultaneously an act of deep compassion, and one of judgement. Yahweh gathers them, gives and guarantees them a place and a name, because Israel cannot be trusted to do so. But this is the wideness of God's mercy: it overrides, sets aside, nullifies the widest judgement of human beings. And if Yahweh gathers, who are we to scatter? If Yahweh includes, who are we to exclude?

Of course, it begs the question: why this shift? Why this dramatic, life-giving change? Why this redemptive rebellion by the liberator-God? I think it is because between Isaiah 51 and 52, and Isaiah 54 and 56, stands Isaiah 53, the song of the suffering Servant. The suffering Servant, the One who had no form or majesty that we should look at him. The One despised and rejected by others, a man of sorrows and acquainted with grief, from whom we all hid our face, because we held him of no account. We would not look at him.

The suffering Servant, crushed and wounded, afflicted by God for our sake, cut off from the land of the living, his life an offering for our sins although we reject him, even as he bears our infirmities and carries our diseases; even as he endures the punishment that made us whole.

The suffering Servant whom the New Testament identifies as Jesus Messiah – it is he who stands between. God chose him and called him 'my beloved Son, in whom I am well pleased'. God raised him from the dead and gave him a name above all names, so that before him 'every knee shall bow and every tongue confess him Lord'. That name guarantees the eternal name that Yahweh gives to the outcasts, a name that is better than sons and daughters. So because of this Name, sons and daughters shall no longer determine a person's worth, their life, or their legacy. Because He was 'cut off from the land of the living', the one who believes upon that name shall never be cut off.

Because of him, no one shall ever be despised; because of him, no one shall ever be rejected; because of him, no one shall ever be an outcast; because of him, we shall all be called, and be named children of God, if we love Him, if we are joined to the LORD, if we keep his Sabbaths and choose the things that please him.

Because of him, they shall all be 'gathered'. And, let me say it again, the criteria Yahweh lays down are not that they be 'changed', made acceptable, made more tolerable, conform, but that they keep his Sabbaths, choose the things that please him and hold fast to his covenant.

It is no wonder that Jesus, in his devastating judgement on the temple and on those who derived their power from the temple's exclusionary powers, calls to his listeners' attention this very passage from Isaiah 56 (Mark 11:15-19). The compassion of the suffering servant seeks justice and inclusion, not only for sinners and prostitutes, but also for strangers and eunuchs; all those, says Calvin, who were excluded from the temple, despised and rejected, deemed outside of the circle of God's grace. Jesus makes clear: justice is inclusion.

VI

So what can we say about Doug? Kathleen, who was your son?

Was he kind, gentle, gifted, friendly, gay? Yes all of that. Nay, more than that. He was, above all, a child of God, uplifted, made whole by the suffering Servant. His presence helped us to be the people of God, restored our own identity. He helped us to know who we truly are. By including him we know we shall not be cut off from the Covenant. His name is written in the palm of God's hand, he is memorised in the church and in our hearts. So within our hearts and in this church he is a *yad vashem*, a wall, a monument, a name, raised to the glory of God, better than sons and daughters.

For that we celebrate his life; for that we memorialise his presence among us; for that we praise God.

Glory be to the Father, and to the Son, and to the Holy Spirit, now and forever more.

When Loveless Power meets the Power of Love

In the time of King Herod, after Jesus was born in Bethlehem of Judea, wise men from the East came to Jerusalem asking, 'Where is the child who has been born king of the Jews? For we have observed his star at its rising, and we have come to pay him homage. When King Herod heard this, he was frightened, and all Jerusalem with him; and calling together all the chief priests and scribes of the people, he inquired of them where the Messiah was to be born. They told him, 'In Bethlehem of Judea; for so it has been written by the prophet: 'And you, Bethlehem, in the land of Judah, are by no means least among the rulers of Judah; for from you shall come a ruler who is to shepherd my people Israel.' Then Herod secretly called for the wise men and learned from them the exact time that the star has appeared. Then he sent them to Bethlehem, saying, 'Go and search diligently for the child; and when you have found him, bring me word so that I may also go and pay him homage.' When they had heard the king, they set out; and there, ahead of them, went the star that they had seen at its rising, until it stopped over the place where the child was. When they saw that the star had stopped, they were overwhelmed with joy. On entering the house, they saw the child with Mary his mother; and they knelt down and paid him homage. Then, opening their treasure chests, they offered him gifts of gold, frankincense and myrrh. And having been warned in a dream not to return to Herod, they left for their own country by another road.

Matthew 2:1-12

I

Matthew 2 is one of those chapters that so powerfully demonstrates the richness of the Bible. There are so many ways of looking at this text. From one point of view, Matthew 2 is the jubilant announcement of the universality of the Christian faith, the all-inclusiveness of God's love. The wise men come, representing the whole world; that world which did not know, but longed to know. Those outside Israel who knew nothing of Israel's God or of what this God has done for them, are about to discover just how great the great deeds of Israel's God are. They represent that world which did not really understand, but somehow knew that 'something was up'. That world that did not know the answer, but was wise enough to know the question: 'Where is the child who has been born king of the Jews?' While the temple in Jerusalem had become a place where so many felt excluded: women, outcasts, strangers, whoever was considered unclean, the stable in Bethlehem flung wide open the doors of God's kingdom. It's no wonder that it is Matthew who devotes a whole chapter to Jesus' holy rage against the temple establishment who failed to understand the fundamentals God had put in place (Matthew 23). Christmas, Matthew is saying, is the celebration of God's inclusiveness.

Matthew 2 also tells of the death of the innocents, and in so doing reveals the dark side of Christmas. It is a sober, and sobering, insight into the workings of loveless power, power for power's sake. In Matthew's version, angels do not light up the heavens with their presence, do not split the skies with the glory of their singing. Here, they are messengers who bring warnings in the night. In Matthew's story, the 'fear' of Herod is completely different from the fear of the shepherds, filled not with wondrous awe but with dark foreboding. Matthew knows nothing of the 'great joy for all the people' that so permeates Luke's Christmas story. No one goes home 'glorifying and praising' God for all they had seen and heard. Instead, his story is dominated by fear, deceit, flight, murder.

Instead of bringing 'glad tidings of great joy', Matthew sounds a solemn warning: this is always the way the world responds to the presence of God. The loveless powers of the world cannot abide the presence of the power of love. But the world does not, cannot, take on God. So instead it avenges itself on God's defenceless children. Literally. And it has no compassion; it knows no mercy. Because the presence of Jesus exposes the falsehood of earthly power, its insecurity, its weakness and deceitfulness, it cannot but show its real nature: it responds with violence. Matthew is saying this is the way it always will be; followers of this Jesus, beware. And so the 'Glory to God in the highest', so gloriously sung by the angels is completely drowned in the tears of Rachel, subdued by the wailing and loud lamentation of the one weeping for her children and who refuses to be consoled.

We can discover yet another layer of this text. When Matthew frames the birth of Jesus with the violence and destruction that befall the innocent, and ends the life of Jesus with the violence of the cross, he tells us just how much violence in and of itself is violence against God. The murder of the infants foreshadows the death of Jesus. Violence, Matthew tells us, is the inescapable consequence of human sinfulness. Sin is not just rebellion against God; it is violence against God. In all its forms, violence is sin's most authentic expression. Every act of violence is an assault upon our God-given humanbeing-ness, an assault upon the holiness of God. And Jesus gives it no quarter, no place to hide, no room for pretence: even anger and insult is violence, 'liable to judgement', the same as murder (Matthew 5:22).

Matthew tells us something else. In his view, the violence that threatens the life of the world emanates from the centres of power: at Jesus' birth, it is the palace. Right through Jesus' life, it is the temple. At Jesus' death, it is the palace (Herod and Pilate), and the temple (scribes, lawyers and high priests). In this world, power and destruction, power and corruption, power and death always go together. In the world, power is the defeat of humanity because it is always abused. The power of the world is the power of violence: it wreaks havoc upon the earth, and in the lives of the weak, the poor and the powerless. The pride, the arrogance and the greed of those who occupy those centres of power are always a threat to peace and life. The power of Jesus is the power of love. It is the power to serve, to give, to share. It is the power not to crush others in order to survive, but the power to lose oneself so that others may live. It is the power not of callous calculation, but the power of compassionate commitment. It is the power of the cross. The confrontation between these two is the essence of Christian marturia.

Finally, (but what is 'final' in a book so rich?) Matthew chapter 2 makes the same point as does Luke chapter 2, but in a more subtle way: the birth of Jesus spells out God's preferential option for the poor. The stable, not the palace, is the birthplace of this king. The magi were evidently wealthy men, but they had to come to the stable and identify with the poor in order to find the child they were looking for. Luke's story focuses directly on the poor: Mary, Joseph, the shepherds. Matthew's story, by focusing on the magi, raises the question: how shall the rich be saved? And gives the answer: by coming to the stable, by kneeling down in the dirt before the manger, among the animals; by recognising in that child, that poor child of poor parents, the wonderful counsellor, the mighty God, the everlasting Father, the Prince of peace. And it is there, with the child who will give his life that the rich will find their life, acknowledging that this is where God is always to be found.

II

But we are so mesmerised by the magi, so horrified by Herod, that we are in danger of missing a vital point Matthew wants to make. And this is the point I invite you to discover with me. It is the story of the birth of Jesus Messiah, true, but the story is dominated by the actions of Herod. It is the story of Jesus' birth, but the name of Jesus is mentioned only once; the name of Herod is mentioned nine times.

Just as Luke begins his story with 'the days of Caesar Augustus', Matthew places the birth of Jesus 'in the time of King Herod'. It is not just a point of historical interest. There are all sorts of problems with historical figures and events in the gospels, although it is certain that Matthew is speaking of Herod the Great. But the issue at stake is political and theological, rather than historical. The birth of this child cannot be divorced from the political situation of his people. His life will have a profound political impact on his people. Immediately, there is the King of the Jews over against the king of the Jews. The implication is clear: they cannot both be king. As Jesus draws his first breath in this last year of Herod's reign, the battle lines are already drawn.

Jesus was born into a colonised people, ruled by strangers, conquered, afraid, bowed down, oppressed. Overrun, overtaxed, over-burdened. Stripped of honour, dignity and hope, they lived their lives between submission and rebellion, their resentment of their oppressors boiling over every now and then into a revolt, only to be ruthlessly crushed by the Romans.

The surrogate king of the Romans in Judea was Herod, not the choice of the people but trusted by the Romans and with typical arrogance foisted on the people by the Romans. They needed a figurehead, but one who would be as harsh in his rule as any Roman – and he was. Herod was a prime example of the man with power but without authority; a king whose slobbering submissiveness to Rome was matched only by his relentless cruelty toward his subjects. A typical potentate of the ancient near East, his reputation was one of utter ruthlessness. Enraged at his favourite wife, Herod had had her strangled. Had had two of his innocent sons executed, and another one murdered even as he lay on his deathbed. It is said that the emperor had made the comment, 'Better to be one of Herod's pigs, than one of his sons'. He was determined to remove every threat to his own throne.

Here was a man without a conscience, sense of justice, or any trace of humaneness. A ruthless tyrant whose 'greatness' not only reflected his cultural feats, but even more his willingness to ruthlessly crush anyone who got in his way. This, more than anything, has always been the hallmark of earthly power: the willingness to use violence to stay in power, to display the authority one does not have, to enforce the respect one craves but is never given. While my family and I resided in the United States, one 'liberal' newspaper voiced the opinion that President Clinton has to attack Iraq in order to prove what the paper called his 'presidential authority'. The 'greatness' of nations is not measured by their desire for justice and peace but by their ability to destroy. From where we stand today, looking at history, there is no irony at all in the name 'Herod the Great'.

This was Herod, king of the Jews, that most dangerous of persons: a man who trampled upon his people while bowing and scraping to those to whom he owed his power. A king with power, but without legitimacy. A king with power, but without authority. Politics with power, but without soul. So right at the start, Matthew's gospel raises the question: what happens when the kingdom of God enters the world in which men like Herod are king? What happens when loveless power is confronted by the power of love?

III

Matthew structures his story around several crucial announcements, all involving Herod.

Verse 1: 'In the time of King Herod ... .'

Verse 3: 'When King Herod heard ... .'

Verse 7: 'Then Herod secretly called [summoned] ... .'

Verse 16: 'When Herod saw ... he was infuriated ... and he sent and killed all the children ... .'

Verse 19: 'When Herod died ... .'

To my mind, these words unlock the meaning of the story. Each announcement about the king brings us closer to the heart of the matter. 'The time of King Herod' means 'while Herod was in charge'. He was on the throne, the power was his. It was, in a very real sense, his time. When King Herod heard, he got frightened, 'and all Jerusalem with him ...'. They knew that the fear of the powerful was a fearful thing to behold. They knew that when the king is frightened, somehow they will have to pay the price. Even their privileged position as Jerusalem's aristocracy would not protect them from his wrath. For make no mistake: 'all Jerusalem' here does not mean all those little people of Israel, the peasants of the land and the poor of the city, what the Bible calls the *am ha'aretz*. They, the oppressed masses, the excluded and the marginalised, have felt the wrath of the king all along. They would only be too happy if someone should come to challenge the powers that reigned, to bring release, peace and justice.

They were still waiting for the fulfilment of the words of Isaiah:

> See, a king will reign in righteousness, and princes will
> rule with justice … Each will be like a hiding place from
> the wind, a covert from the tempest, like streams of
> water in a dry place, like the shade of a great rock in a
> weary land … (32:1, 2).

And then, that promise that every person longing for justice holds as precious and which has become the greatest wish of the true democrat in every modern nation, as we are forced to endure the mealy-mouthed hosannas and sycophantic paeans sung to the most murderous, war-mongering, incompetent, and dishonest politicians who are called 'world leaders':

> A fool will no longer be called noble, nor a villain said to
> be honourable … (v.5).

No, 'all Jerusalem' are those who knew that their positions of power and privilege, were also threatened by the arrival of this new king. Their time was Herod's time, and his days were numbered. Already it is clear: this Jerusalem the Messiah cannot call home. As it was at his birth, so it will be all through his life and at his death: a city of conflict, a place of rejection, where he will find his death. A city to cry for. Hence the intense longing in the New Testament for the city, designed and built by God, the new Jerusalem, 'prepared as a bride beautifully dressed for her husband' (Revelation 21:1), a place Peter poignantly describes as a new heaven and a new earth, 'where righteousness is at home' (2 Peter 3:13).

The king summoned the wise men, in order to deceive, to find a way of getting rid of the child. When the king saw that he was tricked, frustrated in his plans, he got exceedingly angry. Note how all this is connected with his power. His fear frightens the people, his summons dared not be ignored, even if it is a pack of lies, and even if it implicated the innocent in his plans of murder, and even if his anger causes death.

But this is juxtaposed with different words:

Verse 1: '… Jesus was born … .'

Verse 9: '… and there, ahead of them, went the star that they had seen at its rising, until it stopped over the place where the child was.'

Verse 10: '… they were overwhelmed with joy.'

Verse 11: '… they saw the child … .'

Verse 13: '… an angel of the Lord appeared … .'

This is how I see it. Follow me if you will. Herod was king, but Jesus is born, and with him the challenge to Herod's kingship, and this will be a challenge like none Herod has ever seen. The king sought to implicate the magi by deceiving them, by undermining their worshipful intentions by his intentions of murder, but as they left him, there was the star, the same star they had seen at its rising, the star they identified as the Child's star. And its course, in spite of the interruption by the palace, remained firm: 'until it stopped over the place where the child was.' They saw the star as it kept on moving past the palace, and they knew for certain: this palace, this place of fear, misused and abusive power, this place of intrigue and murder and death, is not His place. His place is elsewhere. Not Jerusalem, but Bethlehem. Herod saw a way to derail God's plans, but the wise men saw the star.

In the palace there was fearful anger and political intrigue. In spite of awesome power backed by the most powerful empire on earth, and surrounded by the religious trappings of divine sanction, the palace was a dark place, driven by the grim determination of a king whose survival depended on his utter ruthlessness. It was a place where enormous wealth bred enormous greed and they kept on feeding on each other. It was a place where bloated power sat on a throne awash with blood. It was a place where compassion was a fatal weakness and where joy had no place. For this reason verse 10 is so utterly startling: when they left *that* place, and came to Bethlehem, 'they saw the child, and were overwhelmed with joy'. While in Luke's gospel the joy is irrepressible and omnipresent, from the baby in Elizabeth's womb to the words of the Magnificat, to the song of the angels to the shepherds as they rushed to and from Bethlehem; Matthew mentions the word only once. And he has to wait ten verses to do it. Only once, but it has the same weight as that Name he also uses only once: Jesus. If there is any joy to be found in this story, *he* is it. Johann Sebastian Bach saw it well.

The magi saw the king, yes. They saw his power, they *felt* it as it smothered all life in the palace and in Jerusalem; they smelled the fear as it hung around the throne. *But they saw the child.* And that changed everything. Herod had carefully laid his plans, the threat would be eliminated, the throne would be secured, his palace would be safe again. And the plan was as cold as it was efficient: simply kill all the children in that age group. But God had plans too. The child would live, for the child is the life of the world. So 'an angel appeared to Joseph …'.

What all this means is simply this: God is in control. Herod may be king, but God is in control. In spite of Herod's domination of the story, God is in control. The Christmas story is not Herod's story, even if it seemed so for a little while, it is God's story. It is not the story of the supremacy of the powerful, it is the story of the vindication of the powerless. The Christmas event is not a lamentation of darkness, despite the tears of Rachel; it is the celebration of the coming of the light. It is not about the power of the throne, it is about the power of love. It is not about the power to deceive, but the power to save. It is not about the power to kill, but the power to give life.

So Matthew does not miss the joy, as we might at first be tempted to think; but in his story it is a joy given birth through pain. It is a joy we can have only when we have walked through the valley of the shadow of death. We truly understand the light of the star only when we have seen the darkness of the palace. And that too, is life. That is what Matthew is at pains to tell us. Only those who weep with Rachel, can truly sing with the angels.

IV

Only it seems as if it never stops. Every Christmas we go to Bethlehem and are forced to ask the question: what difference does it make? It seems as if Herod is still in charge. All around us the hallmarks of his regime abound. There is injustice and exploitation, poverty and deprivation; the power of the powerful is still the power to destroy and the ability to get away with it. The suffering of the innocent continues, even the murder of the children does not stop: ask the children in Bosnia and Serbia; see the children in Liberia and Rwanda, in Burundi and Sierra Leone. See the victims of the new economic injustice in South Africa where the future of our children is bartered for the comforts of the new elite, and where the murderers of children are given state money to defend themselves before the Truth Commission and in the courts. And are found innocent. See the children of America's inner city poor, the victims of drug sales by the CIA and welfare reform policies by Congress. The worst is, I think, what even Herod could not foresee: that it is now the children who are killing the children. In the wars raging across the world, a Unicef report tells us that more than a quarter million children in their teens are the soldiers holding the guns.

Herod is still on the throne. Rachel weeps.

No wonder our lives are full of painful riddles, our faith is a mockery to the world, and we are overwhelmed, not by joy, but by confusion and hurt, surrounded by death. But like with Rachel, our protest against Herod must be our refusal to be comforted. Our refusal to accept things as they are, our refusal to accept that we are powerless to do anything. Rachel's wailing is a rage against the outrage against the children, and it must become ours, until we too, receive 'the reward for our work'. Until we, too, hear the voice of the LORD: 'There is hope for your future' (Jeremiah 31).

It is at this point that we must go back to Matthew's story, for he is not finished yet. We must not forget verse 19, where Herod's name is mentioned for the eighth time. 'When Herod died …'. It is an almost laconic remark. Laconic, but heavy with import. It is more than an announcement for Herod's obituary. It is the answer to the anguished cry of God's people: 'How long, LORD?' It is the comfort for the suffering people of God that the prophet understood so well:

'In a short while … the meek shall obtain fresh joy in the LORD, the needy will rejoice in the Holy One of Israel. For the tyrant shall be no more.' (Isaiah 29:17, 19, 20)

That is the ultimate truth: Herod died, but the child lives.

The child is forced to flee in the middle of the night, but he lives.

He is scorned and rejected, but he lives.

He is falsely accused, but he lives.

He is brought before Pilate, and mocked by yet another Herod, but he lives.

He is deserted by his own, denied and betrayed by those who said they loved him, but he lives.

He was condemned to death, and nailed to a cross, but he lives.

He was buried in a grave, but he rose from the dead and he lives.

He lives, and he has promised, 'I am with you, always, to the end of the world'.

Herod the king is dead, Jesus, the King of kings, is alive. The meek, whom Herod exploited and oppressed, shall inherit the earth, and they shall obtain 'fresh joy' for the tyrant is no more. That 'greatness' that Herod bought for himself by using the taxes of the poor to build splendid palaces and pagan temples, all of that is gone. The child he could not kill, lives, and he lifts the poor from the dust of the earth. That awesome power that Herod craved, and had – all that is gone. The child died, rose and lives, and before him every knee shall bow, even Herod's.

So in the end, Matthew's sober tale is turned into a shout of joy: Herod is dead. Jesus is alive. Hallelujah!

Finders Weepers; Losers Keepers

Do not think that I have come to bring peace on the earth; I have come not to bring peace, but a sword. For I have come to set a man against his father, and a daughter against her mother, and a daughter-in-law against her mother-in-law; and one's foes will be members of one's own household. Whoever loves father or mother more than me is not worthy of me; and whoever loves son or daughter more than me is not worthy of me; and whoever does not take up the cross and follow me is not worthy of me. Those who find their life will lose it, and those who lose their life for my sake will find it.

Matthew 10:34-39

I

Have you noticed how God has a way of turning things on their head? It's not just that God does the unexpected. God does the opposite of what we expect, of what we regard as logical. In Old Testament times, it was logical, and therefore expected, that the eldest son would receive the father's blessing. Not so in Israel. Not Esau, but Jacob, not Manesseh, but Ephraim receives the blessing. Not Reuben is chosen, but Joseph, not the oldest but the youngest son of Jesse, David, is chosen as king. Hagar, the young slave woman, receives a promise as eternal as the promise to Abraham. And then God turns it around again: Esau, the 'rejected' one, turns out to be a better person than Jacob, the 'chosen' one. It causes all sorts of problems and it upsets lives mightily; it goes against custom and convention, it breaks traditions held as sacred. But that is the way this God works. People never get used to it; even those whom God has chosen in this way. It is, in short, the inverted order of the kingdom of God.

When Jesus comes, he is no different. His whole life, from his birth to his resurrection, is a proclamation of this inverted order. It is the poor, not the rich, whom he calls 'blessed', happy. To the rich he says, 'Woe unto you!' We are blessed, Jesus says, when people hate us, exclude us, revile us, defame us, persecute us. Instead of getting angry, or feeling depressed or afraid, we are told to 'rejoice in that day, and leap for joy' (Luke 6:22, 23). To be sure, those of us who are not rich, who feel ourselves reviled and persecuted, have no problem with this. We could live with this inverted order. Especially if Jesus tells us, '...the first shall be last, and the last first.'

But the Bible has a way of turning us on our heads. Our expectations do not automatically fall so neatly in line with God's, and any smugness is totally inappropriate. We all know the saying, 'Finders keepers; losers weepers.' It is logical, it makes sense, it is the wisdom of convention, and therefore, we think, true. Our text this morning turns that around. In the words of Jesus our wisdom is turned upside down: those who find their life, shall lose it; those who lose their life, will find it. Finders, weepers; losers, keepers.

Matthew chapter 10 is not, as we have been told so often, about the 'mission of the twelve'. These words of Jesus are not instructions on how to behave on the 'mission field', specially set out for those who feel 'called to preach the gospel to the heathen'. Matthew 10 is much more than just the favourite text at 'mission conferences', more than just a 'well of comfort' whenever missionaries feel themselves unappreciated, undervalued and underpaid. Neither is it the proof text for what European philosopher Theodore Reik called 'social-masochistic traits' in the Christian faith. It is about the hard truths about following Jesus, an honest and sober reflection on the cost of discipleship.

The language is stark. 'See, I am sending you out like sheep into the midst of wolves ... beware of them'. There are enemies out there and they don't play! They will 'hand you over ... and flog you ...'. There is talk of being 'dragged' before councils and governors and kings (10:16-18). In other words, the conflict will not just be a religious one, it will be political. The challenge of the gospel is not a private, religious issue, it has serious political implications. The confrontation is not just to be with the synagogue, but with society as a whole.

Following Jesus will have consequences for all of life, personal as well as societal. Twice Jesus warns about the tensions that will arise within one's own family, and again the language is alarming. Jesus speaks of 'betrayal' of brother by brother, parents and children. And it is not just betrayal that hurts, it is betrayal 'to death'. So, no less than three times in six verses, Jesus exhorts them not to be afraid. 'Have no fear of them', (v. 26), 'Do not fear ...' (v. 28), 'So do not be afraid ...' (v. 31). And why should they not fear, even when they know there is every reason to be afraid? Because 'there is nothing secret that will not become known' (v. 26); because one should 'rather fear him who can destroy both body and soul in hell'(v. 28); and because 'you are of more value than many sparrows.' (v. 31)

What all this exactly means I cannot easily explain. But this is what I believed it meant all those many times I was reviled, defamed and persecuted, my peace of mind shattered, or when my life was in danger. This is how I understand especially those intriguing words from verse 26, 'there is nothing secret that will not become known'. Trust me, Jesus says, for whatever they do to you will become known, not to the world maybe, but to God. God knows what they do. And unlike the world, when God knows, God will act on your behalf. God knows, and history, now written by the conquerors and the powerful will be uncovered, exposed, corrected and rewritten by God. The truth now crushed to earth will rise again. The cries of the people, their suffering and pain now suppressed and ignored, their voices now silenced, will be heard by God. And the deeds of the godless, their twisting of the truth, their devastation of justice, their glorification of the violence that kept them powerful? It will be seen, in all its ugliness, revealed in all its nakedness, and made into nothing by God. For nothing will be kept secret. So what you are whispered in the ear; the truth so devastating and therefore so offensive that it cannot bear to see the light of day, shout it from the rooftops, even if it costs you a price, for one day God will uphold that truth and prove you right. And that is the truth that makes you free.

But also: that 'whisper' is a reminder of our prophetic calling. When we hear the prophets say, 'Thus says the LORD', they are literally saying, 'Thus the LORD whispered in my ear'. What Jesus is talking about is the prophetic calling of those who follow him. Call out my truth, proclaim my Word, shout it from the rooftops for all to hear. Bring to light their deeds, for God will be your vindication. Trust me, says Jesus, the fear of God, which is the love for God, drives out all fear of human beings. If you love me, you will be strongest at those moments when you think you are weakest. Trust me, Jesus says, because even if what happens to you is not what I want, nothing that happens, will happen without me.

We have often taken verse 29 that reads, '... Yet not one of them will fall to the ground without your Father', to read, as so many translations do, 'Not one of them will fall to the ground without the will of your Father.' But that's not what it says. The Bible never says that it is the will of God that will be reviled, or persecuted, or tortured, or defamed, or killed. That is the will of evil, and of those who do the evil one's bidding. So it does not say that. It says this: you might fall, others may cause you to fall, but if that happens, I will be with you. You will never be alone. And because I am with you, I will share your pain and suffering, I will turn your fear into faith, and as with Job, I will set the boundaries of their power. And because I am with you, I will turn the evil they have intended into good, as I did with Joseph.

For many this is hard to follow, and certainly too hard to believe. For many this is cold comfort; far too shaky a shelter for the intensity of the tempest. But if persecution is not a word one has to look up in a dictionary in order to know what it means, and you have no name in the streets, and prison is not a symbol for your captured soul but in fact a building with walls and bars; when torture is not a state of mind but pain in the body; when exile is not a metaphor but a place, you will be surprised how real this comfort is.

So, do not be afraid. Trust me. But at the same time, Jesus is brutally honest. If you follow me, this will happen. No ifs, buts, or maybes about it. For '... see, I am sending you out like sheep into the midst of wolves ...'. The image is graphic, not open to misunderstanding, not subject to multiple interpretations. If you cannot take the isolation, don't follow me. If you cannot stand being reviled, if your name is too precious to you, don't follow me. If your family is too important to you, don't follow me. If you love a peaceful life, don't follow me. If conflict for the sake of truth bothers you, don't follow me. If you love father or mother, son or daughter more than you love me, don't follow me. A disciple is not above the teacher, Jesus says, what happens to me, will surely happen also to you. 'Are you able to drink the cup that I am about to drink?' Jesus asks at another time (Matthew 20:22).

But of course Jesus is not talking about conflict for conflict's sake. He is not calling all those who simply 'love a good scrap'. Jesus is not speaking of the conflict that arises from our arrogance, our propensity to 'stand on our rights', our tendency to humiliate others in our quest for self-justification. Jesus speaks of the conflict, the suffering that arises from the claim of the truth of the gospel on your life. Three times in this passage he says it: 'Because of me ...' (v. 18); 'Because of my name' (v. 22); 'For my sake ...' (v. 39). It all points away from us. It is not us, but the name of Jesus that is at stake here. We are driven, not by our own arrogance, nor by our own interests, but by the truth of the gospel, and we have to know the difference. And that is hard.

And sometimes the conflict is not with the world who hates us because it hates Jesus. Sometimes it is a confrontation with those who, like us, say they love Jesus. Such was the conflict between Paul and Peter in Antioch. 'But when Cephas came to Antioch' we read, 'I opposed him to his face ...'. The issue was the unity of the church, the equality of all believers, the inclusiveness of the church. Peter refused to eat with Christians from the Gentiles, because he did not want to offend the Jewish Christians, who wanted to keep their 'separateness', their chosenness above others, even in the church. For Paul, this was the height of hypocrisy, (a word he uses twice in one sentence), a defamation of Christ, a denial of what the church was called to be. It was an attack on 'the truth of the gospel' (Galatians 2:14). In Christ all are one, no Jews or gentiles, no slaves or free persons, for all are baptised in Christ. Christ has torn down the dividing wall, 'making us all one'. This truth is so central, so much the heart of the church, that to tamper with it, to deny it, to water it down, is to stand 'self-condemned'. So Peter was confronted 'before them all' (v.14), and Paul is adamant:

> But if I build up the very things that I once tore down, then I am a transgressor ... I have been crucified with Christ; and it is no longer I who live, but it is Christ who lives in me. (vv. 18, 20)

The central issue, however, is not Paul or Peter:

> We ourselves are Jews by birth and not Gentile sinners ... . (v. 15)

Rather the issue is Christ 'who loved me and gave himself for me ...'. If Paul should keep silent, allow Peter and the other Jews 'who joined him in this hypocrisy' to go unchallenged, it would do much more than tear the church apart:

> … Then Christ would have died for nothing … . (v. 21)

Such is the depth of the conflict for the sake of Christ.

III

But we must know something else. Verse 39 is not about sacrificing our life, dying for the sake of Christ. That issue is dealt with in verse 28. Verse 31 tells us not to be afraid even when that happens, and ends that discussion. Verse 32 starts a new section and raises a new issue. The passage that ends with verse 42 and includes our text does not begin with verse 34, but with verse 32.

'Everyone therefore who acknowledges me before others, I also will acknowledge before my father in heaven; but whoever denies me before others, I also will deny before my Father in heaven.'

These words are followed by the warning that Jesus did not come to bring peace but a sword, in other words, strife. Then comes the second warning of tension in the family because of his name, 'a man against his father, and a daughter against her mother'; ending with the sobering, 'Whoever loves father or mother more than me is not worthy of me …'. Verse 40 then continues, 'Whoever welcomes you, welcomes me …'.

This whole passage is not about dying, it is about living. But it's about living a life, not for myself, but for Christ. It's about living a life that I have given up trying to control. And keep and safeguard. It means giving up living my life the way I want it, the way I have planned it. What most of us want, what we all want, is a life: well-planned, safe, with a minimum of risk and pain, secure, peaceful, meaningful, with as little conflict and strife as possible. A life we can control, and plan.

Certainly, that is the way I wanted my life. But that is not always what God has in mind for us. Sometimes, God calls us to a life not filled with peace, a life full of turmoil and strife, a life filled with

---

conflict and uncertainty. It is a life in which we are torn between our love for God and our desire for peace and security; a life torn between what we know we need and what we know God wants. And if we are serious about God, it is not an issue of difficult choices. The truth is we have no choice at all. Because with the alternative we have no life at all.

That is what Jesus means. That is what happens if we lose our lives for Christ's sake.

So our tendency is to keep it. To hold onto our life for dear life. Our deepest, most natural desire is to keep it for ourselves, shape it with our hopes, fill it with our dreams, mold it with our aspirations. And we have the best of reasons: we deserve it, we paid our dues, made our sacrifices. Or, we do it for the children: they deserve it. Life is so short: it is not a dress rehearsal. Self-fulfilment is healthy, modern psychology tells us. And if we are really honest: self-denial is not helpful, neither is it appreciated: no good deed shall go unpunished. There are too many empty spaces from the top when I am not number one.

So we cling on for dear life. We cannot believe that if we give it up we will find it; that when we hold on to it, we will lose it. Keeping control of my own life, is losing it, says Jesus. Giving my life over to God is keeping it. Finders, losers; keepers, weepers.

IV

The chapter from which our text comes, begins with verse 1:

> Then Jesus summoned his twelve disciples and gave
> them authority over unclean spirits, to cast them out,
> and to cure every disease and every sickness.

It ends, not 10:42, but with chapter 11:1, like this:

> Now when Jesus finished instructing his twelve disciples,
> he went on from there to teach and proclaim his
> message in their cities.

This does not simply mean that Jesus did this because, as some commentaries tell us, 'he was not yet finished with his own work'. It really means that even after Jesus had called them, instructed them and given them authority over evil spirits, they still could not do it. That message of Christian discipleship was too hard to take. The *imitatio Christi* calls for far more than the disciples were ready to give at that moment.

And it is hard. I do not blame them. When I was a small boy on my father's knee, I revelled in the stories of the Hebrew Bible, especially the one about Samson, next to David and Goliath, all-time favourites. When I was a young man in the midst of the struggle against apartheid, protesting the evil of racist oppression and marching in the streets for justice, I preached fiery sermons from Exodus and the book of Daniel. In prison I read the Psalms with their ringing call on the 'Judge of all the earth'. Now, at this stage of my life, I think I am beginning to understand Jeremiah.

The picture we have of him is that of an often tormented man, deeply spiritual, intensely aware of his calling by God. Called while still 'in his mother's womb', it is as if he is bound to God and his calling by an umbilical cord. He is shamed, rejected by his people and, he feels, forsaken by God. He gives us the feeling that he would rather be doing something else, anything else, than speaking God's word.

> Woe is me, my mother, that you ever bore me – a man
> of strife and contention to the whole land! (15:10)

He hates being a 'contention', does not like his life of conflict, and longs for the unobtrusive normality a prophet can never seem to have. So he feels himself 'enticed' by God, seduced, deceived and overpowered. That same womb which is the place of his calling, he now wishes his grave. The word he must proclaim has cost him: reproach and derision 'all day long'. And yet such is the power of the God who called him and has prevailed:

> If I say, 'I will not mention him, or speak any more in his
> name', then within me there is something like a burning

fire shut up in my bones; I am weary with holding it in,
and I cannot' (Jeremiah 20:9).

He has never had the joy of simple, uncomplicated living. 'I did not sit in the company of merrymakers, nor did I rejoice' (15:17), means that he has never had a childhood, really. All the joy of being a child was denied him, having been called at so young an age, having the responsibilities of a priest since he was only fourteen. And since there is no evidence of his having practised as a priest, it is his prophetic calling he is talking about. He wants a normal life, not to be feared by people, not to be seen as a threat, and hence avoided like the plague, and yet he knows he cannot have it. God has something else in mind for his life. And it tears him apart. No wonder the words of God, a 'joy' and 'the delight' of his heart in 15:16, so quickly become the 'weight of your hand' in verse 17, under which he 'sat alone', filled with indignation. And it is this indignation over injustice, and his people's peace with it; over their disobedience to God and their indifference to it; over their inability to see what will come of it; it is this that sets him apart, that makes him a threat. The loneliness of this man is profound.

But it is in losing his life that Jeremiah finds it. He finds that the divine intrusion in his life does not leave him victim to the invasion of evil, but open to the flow of the power of God.

> But the LORD is with me like a dread warrior;
> therefore my persecutors will stumble, and they will
> not prevail. They will be greatly shamed, for they will not
> succeed. … For to [the LORD] I have committed my
> cause. (20:11, 12)

I do not liken myself to Jeremiah, but I do think I understand him. I think I understand something of his rage, I know something of his pain, for I too, knew something of his indignation, and of people's reaction to it. I know something of his loneliness. Very early in my life I have given my life to God. I knew from the time I was five years old that I was called to preach. From almost the very first week after ordination I knew that this ministry could not be separated from God's call for justice. For more than twenty years of my life I have done nothing else, because I knew, and believed, that fighting for justice is not just 'part of' our calling, it is at the very heart of discipleship.

But it was hard. It led me to places I never knew existed, to moments I had no experience of and hope never to live through again, to images I had no words for. And I tried to take my life back, to gain some control, to shape my own destiny, because I could not live with the feeling that I have somehow lost my life to a God who possessed it, but did not protect it. A life of struggle, of risk, of imprisonment, of threats, of pain, of uncertainty, of humiliation – was this not more losing it than keeping it?

I thought it was over, that moment when Mandela came out of jail and our people stood in those long lines to cast the first democratic votes in our country's history. And then came the blow: I was charged with fraud and theft, 'investigated' by the same police whom we fought on the streets; charged by the same Attorney-General's office who charged me with sedition in 1985; to stand trial before a judge appointed by the old apartheid regime; demonised by the same white-controlled media who slandered the struggle and who reviled us for as long as anyone can remember. To stand trial while the managers of apartheid sit in Parliament and the murderers of our children are given amnesty.

Is this a life in the hands of God? Is this how we 'find' it? God knows it: what I did in the struggle I never did for myself. In my moments of deepest despair, I think: if only I had accepted those job offers I received then, that would have taken me out of my country and saved me and my family all this pain. But three times in the 1980s I said 'No'; three times I listened to those who said, 'the struggle needs you'; three times I thought I should stay, because my life was not my own.

Did God spare my life only for this? I sometimes think. Saved me from an assassin's bullet only to let me live in shame? To be known to the world only as a thief and a fraud, a person of no worth. 'It would have been better,' one newspaper wrote, 'if Allan Boesak had died during the struggle.' Is that true? There was a time when I was tempted to think so, for it is easier to die in the cause for justice, than to live like this, *and still be a witness for God*. To live to see your life broken down around you; to see how people gorge themselves on what is left of your honour, your name, your hopes and dreams, your human-beingness, your future – that is a different kind of death.

Now God has brought me to this point again. I have to learn again what it means to give over my life. I must learn what it means to trust God, to believe that if we suffer for the sake of Christ, because of his name, our life may be under attack, but it will not be lost. That if we trust God, we will find it. I have no control over my life now. But I do believe God has a purpose with all this. It is not that I understand what this purpose is. Neither do I want it. But I know that in order to save my life, I will have to lose it, and trust God with it.

Joseph knew about it. He sits on his throne with all that power and all that glory as second-in-command in Egypt holding his silver cup. That cup is not just to drink from, he uses it for divination. That cup has become his life. For in ancient times, that was how the powerful in Egypt sought predictability and control: the diviner would pour oil on the wine or water in a special cup and read from the patterns formed on the surface what the future held. Through this process they sought to manipulate the gods so that their lives could be secure. For Joseph, that cup was his life. He could not trust God anymore. He was God's dreamer, but he was sold, kept as a slave, subjected to the schemes of Potiphar's wife with disastrous results. He was thrown in prison, and there, despite everything, had to stay for two full years because someone he had done a favour for forgot about him once he was outside. Finally out of prison, restored and in a position of power, he is determined to keep his life. He can no longer afford to trust a God who has played havoc with his life.

His deepest desire is to keep control over his life. But he loses it: the power controls him and the dream fades. He creates polices that exploit and oppress the poor of Egypt and rob them of their land. 'As for the people, he made slaves of them,' the writer of Genesis tells us, 'from one end of Egypt to the other' (47:21). Joseph had lost it: he allows his hatred for his brothers to poison and control his life. It is only when he gets off that throne, embraces them and finds reconciliation; in other words when he loses what he held so dear, his power, his feelings of revenge, his self-justification, that he finds his life again.

I do not know the future, but I do know God is faithful. And even if at this moment I see no light, yet I will rejoice in the God of my salvation. For God, the LORD, is my strength, and I will hide in the shadows of his wings.

I have never spoken to you so intensely personally before. I last spoke to a congregation this way twenty years ago, when I was told that my name was on a government-sponsored death list in South Africa. But I speak in this way, because I am encouraged by your love, without which my wife and I would not have survived these last two years. This coming week my family and I will leave you to go back to South Africa, to face those charges. I do not know what will happen now. Those of you who read the media know that I have already been judged and found guilty and I have been deeply touched by your concern and your desire to keep us here, rather than let us go into that uncertain situation. I do not know where and how my life will end up, but I do know that I have tried to do God's will. I know that somehow, through all this, God's name shall be glorified. For the One who said, 'those who lose their life for my sake will find it', is also the One who said, 'All authority in heaven and on earth has been given to me … . And remember, I am with you always, to the end of the age.'

'Now to him who is able to keep you from falling, and to make you stand without blemish in the presence of his glory with rejoicing, to the only God our Saviour, through Jesus Christ our Lord, be glory, majesty, power, and authority, before all time and now and forever. Amen.'

CHAPTER 9

Undisciplined Abundance

That same day Jesus went out of the house and sat
beside the sea. Such great crowds gathered around him
that he got into a boat and sat there, while the whole
crowd stood on the beach. And he told them many
things in parables, saying: 'Listen! A sower went out to
sow. And as he sowed, some seeds fell on the path, and
the birds came and ate them up. Other seeds fell on
rocky ground, where they did not have much soil, and
they sprang up quickly, since they had no depth of soil,
but when the sun rose, they were scorched; and since
they had no root, they withered away. Other seeds fell
among thorns, and the thorns grew up and choked
them. Other seeds fell on good soil and brought forth
grain, some a hundred-fold, some sixty, some thirty. Let
anyone with ears listen!'

Matthew 13:1-9

10

'A sower went out to sow … .' This must be one of the most well-known parables of Jesus, and one of the most difficult to preach on. Not only because everyone thinks there is nothing new to learn, but also because Jesus makes it so hard by giving both the exegesis and the application of this parable. Preachers have to watch out, lest congregations think we are trying to go one better than Jesus. Nonetheless, we should try, otherwise you may have come to church for nothing this morning. But a word of caution is in place here: when we think we know the Bible too well, it is usually a sign that we do not know very much at all, or not nearly enough. Besides, when Jesus begins, and ends, this parable with the emphatic 'Listen!' of v. 3 and v.9, it means that there is more here than meets the ear.

So let us linger a bit. It will be worth our while to find out what this parable is all about and what it is Jesus wants to say to us. Let's get something out of the way first. The parable of the sower is not about evangelism or mission. Nor is it about the Bible Society, although they have made 'the sower' their international emblem and we have no quarrel with that. It is, like all parables, about the kingdom of God. It is about the presence of that kingdom as it bursts onto our worldly scene in the presence of Jesus of Nazareth. It is about the power of that kingdom as we are confronted with it, and our reaction to that power. What happens when the kingdom of God is realized in our midst?

II

There is much that is intriguing about this parable. The most compelling thing is not, I think, the seed and what happens to the seed although I realise that that is what has always captured our attention. What catches my eye is not so much the seed, but the sower. What grabs me is not so much where the seed falls (although that is important also, as we shall see), but why it falls where it falls. What makes me want to take a closer look, are not the birds, the rocks, the path, or the thorns, but rather the behaviour of this sower. Why is he doing what he is doing?

Because his behaviour is, frankly, rather peculiar. The seed falls where it does, because of the reckless abandon, the unchecked generosity, the undisciplined abundance of this sower. The Palestinians who were listening to Jesus in those times were mostly peasant farmers. There were some fisher folk, and a few artisans, but most of them lived off the land. They were poor, but they were not stupid. By the time of Jesus, most of them had lost their land to wealthy landowners through debt and the selfish economic policies of the aristocracy, and what was left were only small parcels of arable land. Rainfall was scarce. What was left over from the previous harvest could not have been much: so caution was the watchword.

Those farmers sitting there, listening to Jesus on that day would never think of doing what that sower was doing in Jesus' story. I remember, as a child, going to my mother's birthplace, a small rural community called Ebenezer on the West Coast, near places like Vredendal, Lutzville and Koekenaap in the Western Cape. Most people there were peasant farmers who lived off the land. So were my uncles. I remember going out with them, watching them plough the land with a plough pulled by a horse. I remember with what precision they made their furrows and how, with even more precision, they carefully sowed the seed into those furrows, taking the seed out of a bag slung over their shoulder.

That was how they did it. Carefully. Joyfully also, for sowing is a wonderful thing, done with so much gratitude for the past and even more hope for the future, but carefully. Wastefulness was not only sinful, it was stupid. That was also how the peasant farmers of Jesus' time did it. What must have caught their attention, as they listened to this parable, was not the rocky ground (there was rocky ground everywhere), nor the thorns, (any farmer worth their salt knows how to avoid that), nor the birds (these were a pest at sowing time anyway), but the sower.

For it was clear to them: this sower was not sowing like he should. Instead of throwing the seed carefully into the furrows, he flung his arms wide, letting the seed fly out of his hand, every which way. As if he didn't have a care in the world. As if, as we say these days, he had seed 'for Africa'. As if there were no such thing as drought, or failed harvests, or scarce land, or precious seed, or careful husbandry. If you sow like that, no wonder the seed would fall on the road, or among thorns, or on rocky ground. But you really had to be incredibly stupid to let that happen.

They would never have done it like that. So why is the sower so wasteful, so undisciplined, so unbelievably generous? Going out there, sowing seed in places where it's guaranteed that nothing will grow?

III

So, who is the sower? The sower is the one who proclaims the 'word of the kingdom'. But ultimately, the sower is God. Only God can be so generous with God's Word. But this word is more than the words of the parable. This word is all the promises of God, for all who want to hear; 'anyone with ears', Jesus says.

All the promises of God, we say, in all of their rich abundance. All the acts of God, in all their sweeping, overwhelming generosity. And let anyone with ears, listen!

> Let us make humankind in our image, according to our likeness; and let us give them dominion …

It is not as if God is sitting in some boardroom making careful calculations, weighing the pros and the cons, checking the balance sheet, considering the risks. 'In our image.' The psalmist understood it well,

> What are human beings that you are mindful of them, mortals, that you care for them? Yet you have made them a little lower than God, and crowned them with glory and honour. You have given them dominion over the works of your hands, you have put all things under their feet … . (8: 4-6)

Such trust, such honour, such boundless confidence in the creatures God has made! I will make you all that I hope you will become, says God. But all you can become, is already there! I will pour my image into you, hoping that you will reflect my likeness. There is no careful bookkeeping here, wondering how much to invest or how to hedge the bets. You can be sure the devil was there somewhere, looking over God's shoulder saying, 'You will regret this'. And of course God would regret this. Of course we would mess it up. Of course we would waste it all. It was but a small jump from Genesis 1 to Genesis 6, and an even smaller jump from Genesis 6 to us. But that does not stop this God. There is no end to the generosity of God when it comes to us.

We have to really hear this. 'I shall be your God and you shall be my people ... .' 'I shall destroy Pharaoh and his armies and I shall glorify my name ... .' And God did it, so that the exodus became the focal point of Israel's faith for all time and the mighty deeds of God's liberation became the foundation of Israel's confession of faith.

'If my people, who are called by my name, humble themselves, pray, seek my face and turn from their wicked ways, I shall forgive them and heal their land ... .' This is not a God of half-measures. God holds nothing back. It is for this reason that the psalmist cannot but respond to this amazing generosity of God,

> Bless the LORD, O my soul, and all that is within me,
> bless his holy name ... . Who forgives all your iniquity,
> who heals all your diseases, who redeems your life ...
> who crowns you with steadfast love and mercy ... .
> (103)

It is the wideness of God's mercy, the boundlessness of God's love, the wholeness of God's actions, that makes the psalmist shout with such unrestrained joy.

And when Jesus appears, he cannot and does not do anything different. 'Come unto me, all you who labour ... all you who are heavy-laden, and I will give you rest ... .' And the most generous of all: 'Your sins are forgiven ...'. And the most comforting of all: 'All authority in heaven and on earth has been given to me ... And remember, I am with you always, to the end of the world ... '.

All of God's promises, for all of our lives, for all of us. This is a generosity that defies all attempts at definition, messes up all the straight lines of human logic, mocks our efforts at description. It simply takes our breath away.

IV

The question is not: do we deserve it? Because we don't. Mostly we tend to think we do, but we don't. We have all but destroyed God's creation, defiled God's image in ourselves and in others, trampling upon their humanbeingness and betraying ours, as if it were nothing. We have burned ourselves up with hatred, lived as if God did not exist, making a living out of our greed and rapaciousness, our love for war and violence and our weakness for destruction.

We do not deserve God's abundance. We act as if we can live without love, as if we do not need repentance, or forgiveness, or reconciliation. Our theology is no more than the religious sanctification of the dominant culture we believe to be our salvation. Max Warren, that great scholar of Christian missions, had captured the dilemma of Western Christianity and made it plain forty-five years ago:

> Our liturgy is the catchwords of the daily press. Our divine revelation is the nine o'clock news. Our creed is 'I believe in democracy'. Our incentive is the fear of – we are not sure what. But it certainly is not the fear of the Lord.

No, the question is not whether we deserve it. The question, rather, is: can we take it? Let me try to make it plain: can we take it – a God who is so generous? Can we live with a God who is so much more generous than we are, nay more, than we can stand God to be? Can we truly worship this undisciplined, merciful God who just gives and gives, as he sows and sows?

For notice how the gospel of Matthew deals with just this theme. At Jesus' birth there are not just the angels who bring heaven down to earth on that wondrous night; there are not just the shepherds who represent the people of Israel, despised though they may have been by the privileged classes; there are also the magi from the East, representing all that unknown world who knew nothing about the God of Israel nor about the King of the Jews about to be born. They too, must share in God's abundant love.

In Matthew's gospel it is not just people who are swept up and away by the greatness of this moment. Something is happening here, so new, so different, so compelling, that even the laws of nature are changed. Stars charter a new course, with a light so bright that the world can navigate their way to the place where the baby was born and find salvation. With that star, the whole universe stands still, in wonder, above 'the place where the baby was born'.

In the Sermon on the Mount, Jesus opens wide the floodgates of the kingdom of heaven so that the stream of mercy flows and flows. Love your enemies, Jesus says. Not just try to like them; or try not to dislike them; or try to survive with them or try to deal with them with the minimum of damage. No, love them. Ask, Jesus says, just ask, and it will be given. Knock, and it will be opened. 'For everyone who asks receives, and everyone who searches, finds, and for everyone who knocks, the door will be opened.' (7: 8)

It is Matthew who tells us of the parable of the labourers in the vineyard (20:1-16). It is through Matthew that we learn of the remarkable ethic of the owner: everyone who comes, it does not matter when, gets paid the same wage. Those who come early in the morning, or those who come an hour before knock-off time, it does not matter: they are all treated equally. The point is clear: in the kingdom of God, it does not matter when someone comes, as long as they come. I do not even want to know what the Congress of South African Trade Unions would have to say about this! Our trade unions would no doubt have Jesus before the Industrial court in no time!

V

But of course, everywhere where this kind of generosity is

demonstrated, there has to be a reaction. Matthew does not try to hide that disturbing fact. After the magi comes the murder of the innocents. The Sermon on the Mount is followed by a series of confrontations with Pharisees and scribes and lawyers that inevitably lead to Jesus' death. Only one chapter later, as he healed two demoniacs in 'the country of the Gadarenes', 'the whole town' came to see him, not to thank him, not to ask his blessing, but to 'beg' him to leave. Such wonderful doings embarrassed them, irked them, irritated them. By the time a paralytic is healed and told by Jesus, 'Your sins are forgiven', outraged scribes and the temple leadership were already thinking 'evil in their hearts'.

Matthew chapter 13, from which our text for this morning is taken, leads us to Nazareth where Jesus was rejected by his own folk, his 'hometown', who could not stand it when he spoke of the generosity of God in their synagogue. They were offended by his words and deeds, angered by a God they could not control and own. Their resentment boiled over. So they had to familiarise him, domesticate him, despise him, so that they could reject him. The reference to Jesus as 'the carpenter's son', and to his mother Mary, his brothers and sisters, is not an expression of neighbourly pride, but rather an attempt at control. If they could only put him in his place, they would not have to deal with his wisdom. 'And he could not do many deeds of power there … .', Matthew writes. Mark is far more brutal. Jesus could not do any works there, Mark says, 'because of their unbelief'.

The generosity of God always, *always* brings a reaction, and in the Bible it is remarkable how negative that reaction is. In Matthew 20, the parable of the workers in the vineyard ends with confrontation. The great generosity of the owner of the vineyard creates an even greater anger. The hopefulness reflected in the words, 'No one has (yet) hired us', is completely overshadowed by the anger of v. 11, '… they grumbled against the landowner …'. It is not the miserly greed of the owner, but the freedom of the owner to do with his own what he wishes, i.e. giving freely, that causes the anger. And in the parable Jesus casts this in the framework of a confrontation between good and evil: 'Is your eye evil because I am good?' (v. 15)

In other words, is the goodness of God so indigestible that the evil of the human heart sees it as evil? And only a few verses further, '… And the Son of Man will be handed over to the chief priests and scribes, and they will condemn him to death'.

So the question remains: can we take it? Can we live with this God whose generosity so far outstrips our ability even to understand? Can we take it, us liberal Christians, so enamoured of our own liberalism that we are embarrassed by the Bible? Can we take it, we who are so sure of our politics but have no confidence in our faith? Can we take this God, we who are too modern and intellectual to believe in evil, yet the devils are all around us: racism, patriarchalism, homophobia, classism, and that frightening, war-loving, self-satisfied Christian nationalism so peculiar to America? And in all these years we, like the disciples of Jesus, 'could not cast them out'.

Can we worship a God who is so open, so ready to accept those to whom we have closed the gates of the kingdom? We have made the church one of the most exclusionary, unmerciful places on earth, locking the doors of God's grace to all whom we deem unsuitable for the kingdom. Can we accept a God whose standards of admission are so much lower than ours? A God who is so judgemental about our tendency to judge, so indiscriminately open-handed where we are so self-righteously close-fisted? We are so frustrated with the Bible because it is not so politically correct, so legally responsible, so deliciously ambiguous as our well-crafted decisions taken at our Synods, Conferences and Assemblies. Next to our theological frugality, our miserly Christian life, this undisciplined, exuberant, spendthrift God of the Bible is an exasperating embarrassment.

Measured by our theological verbosity, the simplicity of the biblical demand, love God, love your neighbour, do justice, love mercy, walk humbly with your God, leaves us totally at a loss. Jesus says, 'Do you love me?'. But because we know it is not so much the simplicity of this demand, but the radicality of its implications that really bothers us, we obfuscate the issue with a zillion questions totally unrelated to the love of God, or justice, or mercy. Never mind walking 'humbly' with God.

And still God sows, and sows, because maybe, God thinks, maybe some seed will fall on fertile ground. And so where the seed falls, matters after all. But are we ready for this? Who would have thought it: we who are sitting here today, we are not so totally overwhelmed by our sinfulness, not so totally corrupted by evil, not so totally unyielding through our hardness of heart, that we cannot respond to what Jesus calls 'the word of the kingdom'. If we will, if only we will, we are able to hear the Word and understand it, bear fruit and yield. Hence the plea in the words of Jesus: 'Let anyone with ears, listen!'.

But this is not all. Do you know what really grabs me in this parable? What I really cannot, as you say in America, 'wrap my mind around'? This: some yield a hundredfold, some sixty, some thirty. And it does not matter! If it yields a hundredfold, that's great. God be praised. If it yields sixty, that's all right too, it does not matter. As long as it yields something. It may not be a hundred, but the point is, it yields something. But some cannot even go that far, they yield only thirty. But you know what? Even that's all right too! Before God, that does not matter. As long as we respond, as long as we yield something. The God who gives the same wages to those who came early as to those who came late, is the God who accepts whatever we are able to give. The same God who is able to multiply the bread and fishes so that five thousand and more could be fed, is able to take our thirtyfold and multiply it into something beyond our abilities and our belief.

I can hear some saying this morning, but Jesus, I am so weak, I try and try, and yet I fail. That's alright! God still sows. I can hear some saying, my mistakes are so great, they have done so much damage. That's alright! God still sows. I can hear some saying, Jesus, I have made such a mess of my life. That's alright too. God still sows! Oh, if we would only take Jesus half as seriously as we take ourselves, we will be astonished, and the world will be astounded, at what the church of Jesus Christ could do.

It is Paul, writing to the Ephesians, who says that if we open ourselves up to the power of the Spirit of God, allow her to work within us, God is then able 'to accomplish abundantly far more than all we can ask or imagine'. Paul has one of the most fertile imaginations I know, and even he cannot imagine what God can do through us, if we give ourselves over to the Spirit. Can we do it? Can we be as generous with others as God is with us? Can we really believe, even as we hear this, that through our generosity, following God's generosity, the world can be utterly, fundamentally, truly and wonderfully changed?

And God sows, with exuberant generosity, with unalloyed, wasteful joy, with undisciplined abundance, in the hope that some seed will fall on fertile ground, yield something, so that God's Word will not return empty.

So let us thank God for being loving, let us thank God for being faithful, let us thank God for being powerful. But above all, let us thank God for being so abundant, so shameless in generosity, so undisciplined in love and mercy and grace. For without that, where would we be? Bless the LORD, O my soul!

The Real Dilemma

When they came to the disciples, they saw a great crowd around them, and some scribes arguing with them. When the whole crowd saw him, they were immediately overcome with awe, and they ran forward to greet him. He asked them, 'What are you arguing about with them?' Someone from the crowd answered him, 'Teacher, I brought you my son; he has a spirit that makes him unable to speak; and whenever it seizes him, it dashes him down; and he foams and grinds his teeth and becomes rigid; and I asked your disciples to cast it out, but they could not do so.' He answered them, 'You faithless generation, how much longer must I be among you? How much longer must I put up with you? Bring him to me.' And they brought the boy to him. When the spirit saw him, immediately it convulsed the boy, and he fell on the ground and rolled about, foaming at the mouth. Jesus asked the father, 'How long has this been happening to him?' And he said, 'From childhood. It has often cast him into the fire and into the water, to destroy him; but if you are able to do anything, have pity on us and help us.' Jesus said to him, 'If you are able! All things can be done for the one who believes.' Immediately the father of the child cried out, 'I believe; help my unbelief!' When Jesus saw that a crowd came running together, he rebuked the unclean spirit, saying to it, 'You spirit that keeps this boy from speaking and hearing, I command you, come out of him, and never enter him again!' After crying out and convulsing him terribly, it came out, and the boy was like a corpse, so that most of them said, 'He is dead.' But Jesus took him by the hand and lifted him up, and he was able to stand.

Mark 9:14-29

11

Life is not simple – it is never easy. It is not just that life is hard. That we know: to keep head above water, to survive another day, to feed our children, to give them more than we ourselves have had. We know that. It is also that life is sometimes so difficult to understand. We cannot figure out God's purposes, we are baffled by God's ways with us. And it does not end there. Life is a constant battle with evil, and while we feel the powers of evil are overwhelmingly strong, we feel ourselves to be pitifully weak. We want to do what is right, but even the good we do is sometimes tinged with darkness. Often our best deeds have sad, unforeseen consequences. Paul's dilemma is our own:

> When I want to do good, evil lies close at hand .... For
> I delight in the law of God in my inmost self, but I see
> in my members another law at war with the law of my
> mind, making me captive to the law of sin that dwells in
> my members ... wretched man that I am!
> (Romans 7:21-24)

Life is not just black and white, it is mostly vast areas of gray, filled with painful dilemmas, by their very nature problems which seem to defy solution. Dilemmas that cause us to get lost, not so much in the dark as in the mist. To our dismay and discouragement, we face dilemmas we cannot even name, let alone overcome.

The gospel story from Mark chapter 9 is a story about dilemmas; a sick child's dilemma, a father's dilemma, the disciples' dilemma. But more specifically, it is about the discovery of the father's real dilemma.

Our story begins, not with verse 14, but with verse 2. Jesus is on the mountain with Peter and James and John. Something quite glorious happens on that mountain. Jesus is anointed by God, and he is transfigured. His clothes became dazzlingly white, his whole being is transformed. Moses and Elijah appear, the two most excellent examples from the Hebrew Scriptures of persons who lived in,

---

and from, their intimate, special relationship with Yahweh. Moses, 'whom the LORD knew face to face', and Elijah, 'Israel's chariots and its horsemen'. Never since their death could anyone in Israel be spoken of thus. Now the legacies of their life, their words, their acts in the name of God for the sake of God's people, their relationship with Yahweh come together in this man from Nazareth, this prophet from Galilee, Jesus, son of Mary and Joseph, and Son of God. And they do not come to legitimise Jesus. They come to rejoice in him.

Then comes the voice from the cloud: 'This is my Son, the Beloved; listen to him!' (v.7). Suddenly they were alone. Moses and Elijah have disappeared. There is only Jesus. At the moment God claims Jesus as God's anointed and proclaims him 'the Beloved' to whom henceforth the world must listen, the focus is no longer on either Moses or Elijah, for from now on both the purifying fire of the Torah and the liberating fire of prophecy will burn in him. And that is the fire he 'came to bring to the earth' (Luke 12:49), which will bring division between mothers and daughters, and fathers and sons. It is the fire that consumes the fig tree and foretells the ruin of the temple. It is the fire that burns when he takes the side of the poor against the rich, when he speaks about the true meaning of the law and denounces scribes and Pharisees (Matthew 23). Hence the gospels call Jesus the 'fulfilment of the Law and the prophets'.

Jesus of Nazareth is not the break with the Law, he is the radical fulfilment of the Law. He does not represent a break with Israel's prophetic tradition, he is the resurrection of the prophetic tradition. Jesus' confrontational engagement with the interpreters of the law and the temple establishment is therefore not just Galilean rebelliousness, the gospels are saying, it is the carrying out of a divine mandate.

The three disciples are terrified, Mark tells us. But clearly this is a terror not fueled by fear, but by excitement. Peter wants to build three huts. Apparently he is not so terrified that he wants to leave as soon as possible. He wants to stay! And I don't blame him. It must have been wonderful, that moment. Not only Jesus, but also Moses and Elijah – who could wish for more? We would also have wanted to prolong that moment.

But Jesus knows: he's got to go down. One cannot stay on the mountaintop forever. On the mountaintop there is communion with God. It is a frightening, but nonetheless glorious experience. But down in the valley lies the world. There, in the world, are people with their pain and suffering, their helplessness and hopelessness. They are in need of someone who knows their pain, who will respond to their pain; someone who can offer them liberation, someone who has heard the voice of God, who has been anointed by God, on whom the Spirit of the Lord rests. They are in need of Jesus. So he has to go down, however good it was on that mountaintop.

We, too, cannot stay on the mountaintop for too long. Sunday morning is followed by Monday morning and we have to face the world again. That world where the joyful 'Yes Lord!' of Sunday morning is pushed aside by the groaning 'Oh Lord!' of Monday morning. We know that we cannot escape that world or act as if it did not exist, with its suffering, its challenges, its dilemmas. That world where we cannot hide, where the demons hold sway, and where our inability to deal with them will be ruthlessly exposed. No, we know: the true terror is not on the mountaintop, where God is present, but down in the world where God is challenged.

III

So Jesus came down. The first thing he saw was the 'great crowd', and the first thing he heard was that an argument was going on. After the mountaintop experience, this must have been a rather depressing sight. Especially in light of what turns out to be the real reason for this unseemly wrangling: the plight of a sick boy.

'What are you arguing about with them?' It is a question of exasperation, not of inquiry. It is a question that highlights our extraordinary human insensitivity, rather than Jesus' desire to know. It is a question that exposes our sinful preoccupation with ourselves, rather than Jesus' ignorance of what really goes on in the minds of sinful human beings. So, in the story there is no real response to the question. We hear nothing of what the debate was all about, because that is not what Mark is interested in. He simply wants to show what we are like: arguing about piffling things while real people's lives are threatened. The sight of this violently ill boy does not invoke the compassionate question, 'What can we do?', but the self-interested question, 'How can we exploit this?' How utterly shameful.

But there is a second point Mark wants to make. When there is a response, we hear nothing of the theological debate that was going on. Nothing about the 'nature of God', or the metaphysical relationship between God and the universe; no philosophical speculation about the meaning of life, or whether God really created the world in six days. Instead, we hear, 'Teacher, I brought you my son …'.

We are plunged immediately into the excruciating dilemma of a parent. The gospel moves directly to our problems. God is not nearly as interested in the correctness of our theological discourse as God is in our life. In the end, our arguments about theology are far less important than our deeds of solidarity and faith. In the end, our doctrinal disputes which we waged with such withering self-righteousness and that cost so many their peace of mind and even more their lives, will be worthless. And it is not as if we did not know this all along:

> Then the king will say to those at his right hand, 'come, you that are blessed by my Father, inherit the kingdom prepared for you from the foundation of the world; for I was hungry and you gave me food, I was thirsty and you gave me something to drink, I was a stranger and you welcomed me, I was naked and you gave me clothing, I was sick and you took care of me, I was in prison and you visited me' … 'Truly I tell you, whatever you did to one of the least … of mine, you did for me … whatever you did not do for one of the least of these, you did not do for me … . Then they will go away to eternal punishment, but the righteous to eternal life.' (Matthew 25:34-36; 45-46).

So Jesus receives no answer. Instead, a father steps forward. 'Teacher, I have brought you my son, who is possessed …'. And that is the reason Jesus has to come down from the mountain, it is the only thing that matters. And now we see also the father's dilemma. But it is a dilemma upon a dilemma. First, his son is ill. An evil spirit possesses him. But secondly, the disciples could not heal him. This parent did not know how to explain his son's illness. Today we might say that the boy was epileptic. But for the people of Jesus' day it was a frightening display of a dark, unknown, hurtful, uncontrollable power. And since the father cannot speak in medical terms, he speaks simply as a father who feels the pain of his child deeply. 'Whenever it seizes him, it throws him to the ground. He foams at the mouth, gnashes his teeth, and becomes rigid.' Clearly the child is in deep distress, and in real danger.

Even as the father speaks, the evil spirit shows his power. 'When the spirit saw Jesus, it immediately threw the boy into a convulsion. He fell to the ground and rolled around, foaming at the mouth.' Mark sets the scene. 'When the spirit saw Jesus.' The spirit tortures the child, but its anger is directed at Jesus. The spirit knows it is no longer facing a victimised child and a helpless parent. From now on, the confrontation is to be between the evil spirit and Jesus. Between the power of life and the power of death. Between the presence of evil and the presence of the kingdom of God. This boy, and his father, are no longer alone. Verse 20, which at first glance reads like a sentence filled with despair, suddenly becomes a sentence filled with hope. The boy is afflicted, therefore God is challenged. You touch this child, God is saying, and you touch me.

But then Jesus does a strange thing. He does not immediately heal the boy, which is the fervent wish of the parent. Jesus first wants a conversation with the father. 'How long has he been like this?' I can well imagine the father's surprised impatience. What is this? he must have thought. Can Jesus not see what is happening before his very eyes? What does it matter how long this has been going on? What matters, surely, is that the boy was ill, and that it is still going on! His immediate disappointment must have been acute, as any parent would understand. Are we to have a discussion while my boy is dying? Does even Jesus not really understand?

It is perhaps for this reason that the father now so painstakingly explains, in great detail, what his son is going through. 'From childhood', he says. That means, all his life. He has never had a life, this child. It means we have tried everything, and no one and nothing helps. Jesus is their last hope. So the father makes sure Jesus understands: 'It has often thrown him into fire or water to kill him.' (v.22). This is the reality of this child's life, and that of his parents. The evil spirit is out to destroy them. The description is grim, and surely not easy for this parent. But he has to say it.

Jesus wants to establish the boy's condition, so that the father can understand his dilemma: his child is ill. It becomes immediately clear, though, that that is only his first dilemma. His second dilemma is that he is powerless, and that the evil spirit is powerful. The boy is its captive. At a deeper level, Jesus wants him to understand that evil is real. Hence Jesus' question, which draws the starker description from the father in verse 22. He holds nothing back: the evil spirit seeks the life of his child. When one puts the boy's condition in those terms, the evil spirit is not just something, it is real.

And that is something us modern Christians, civilised and sophisticated, cannot understand. In fact, we resist any understanding of it since we have relegated this story to the realm of myth and all talk of evil to the lunatic fringes of our own societies and to the simple-minded superstition of bush dwellers.

But evil is real. Everything that agitates against the will of God, that threatens our humanity, that challenges the love of God and seeks to destroy which God has made good and worthwhile, is evil. Everything that is violent and destructive is evil. When we confront lawlessness dressed up as law; inhumanity and brutality parading as law and order; bigotry and racism posing as Christian values, we must know, evil is real.

When we see children dying of hunger while the rich die of over-eating; when there is money for weapons of mass destruction but not for the poor and needy, the weak and elderly, we must know: evil is real. When military budgets dwarf the puny amounts spent on research and development of medicine, evil is real. Evil stands up in the 'hallowed halls of power', making laws that punish the children of illegal immigrants but reward and protect the wealthy companies that bring them into the country as a source of cheap labour. Evil rises up in courts of law, punishes the young black man for using drugs, but leaves alone the rich banks who launder drug money. And evil sometimes stands up in the pulpit, telling God's children that all this is God's will, and that our concern should not be life on earth but our 'eternal reward in heaven'.

It is not for nothing that Paul reminds us:

> For our struggle is not against enemies of blood and
> flesh, but against the rulers, against the authorities,
> against the cosmic powers of this present darkness,
> against the spiritual forces of evil in the heavenly places.
> (Ephesians 6:12)

And it is not for nothing that this is followed almost immediately by Paul's request (twice!) that the church should pray for him, so that he may speak 'boldly'.

Evil is real, and those of us who had come face to face with it, do not smile indulgently at the 'primitiveness' of the gospel. We have only to read the stories of the survivors of Auschwitz, or see the victims of the massacres in Chiapas or Burundi; or hear the stories of the victims of police torture in apartheid South Africa, to know: evil is real. And the sooner we deal with it as a reality, the better it will be.

IV

The father in our story is faced with a dilemma. His son is ill. Evil is real and powerful, that is his second dilemma. But that is not his real dilemma. He brought his son to Jesus, and the disciples could not cast it out. Literally, Mark says, 'They were not strong enough.' The 'strong man' of evil proved to be stronger than they. This must make us pause. Peter, who would declare himself ready to follow Jesus 'even into death' – not strong enough? John and James, 'sons of thunder' – not strong enough? The disciples, the ones specially called by Jesus, and who, just a few chapters before, had been given 'authority over evil spirits' – were they not strong enough? But even that is not his real dilemma, for he knows that beyond the disciples there is Jesus, to whom he now appeals, to whom he now takes his case.

'If you can do anything, take pity on us and help us' (v.22). There are some who take that 'if' as expression of this parent's lack of faith. I think so too, but I don't think we can blame him. After so many years of living on the brink of death, sharing the agony of every waking and sleeping moment of that child's life; after spending who knows how much on doctors who could not give relief; after battling with evil demons they could not hope to overcome; after witnessing the callous point scoring of disciples and teachers of the law; and after seeing the disciples' own helplessness as they were not strong enough to cast out the evil spirit; after all that, who could blame him?

Certainly Jesus doesn't. 'If you can?' Jesus says. We tend to read: 'If you *can*', as if Jesus were debating the possibilities for himself here. But I think we should read, 'If *you* can.' Jesus is placing the onus on the father in an amazing and immediate identification and overturning of the father's lack of faith. It is not Jesus' willingness or unwillingness, but the father's faith that is at issue here. 'If *you* can ... .' Now that you know the seriousness of your son's problem; now that you have given words to the unspeakable; now that you understand the reality of evil; now that you have come to the right person; now it is finally up to you. Jesus has more confidence in this father than he has in Jesus. Jesus calls on the faith he should, but does not, have. And that is this father's real dilemma.

And only when Jesus spells it out: 'All things are possible for the one who believes', only then does the father realise his real dilemma. He understands, and responds immediately: 'I do believe; help my unbelief!' In other words, help me overcome my inability to believe as I should. The real dilemma this man is facing is not his son's illness, not the evil spirit's power, not the disciples' helplessness, nor Jesus' unwillingness. The real dilemma is his unbelief.

V

God does not always answer our prayers immediately. God does not respond with the rapidity we would like. Even though the complexity of our problems is real and our dilemmas undeniable, God's response is not always forthcoming. We are impatient, knowing that our lives, and those of our children, are under siege. God takes time to talk with us until we are clear about what is really happening to us and our children. Until we learn that the state of the world is not an accident, an 'act of God', or 'just the way the cookie crumbles', but the result of human sin, of greed, violence and rapaciousness. Until we see that the situation in which we find ourselves is not just the result of blind fate, the roll of the dice, the turning of the windmills of the gods, but the devastation of the reality of evil. God waits, until we come to see that our deepest problem is not 'the world' and how impossible it is to change it; or 'the church' and how negligent our witness has become; or 'politicians' and how untrustworthy they are.

God waits, until we have discovered our real dilemma: our inability to know evil for what it is, and our lack of faith. And that is the heart of the matter. Our faith. The openness to believe that all things are possible for those who believe. Not just some things, not just the things within our reach, not just the things we think we understand or are able to figure out – *all things*.

But we are perhaps too primitive for that. Because the self-appointed gurus of talk radio have supplanted the voice of the Holy Spirit, and television regulates and dictates our vision, and the newspaper has become our Bible, it is easier for us to believe that all things are possible for those who have power; for those who have money, for those with position and status, or failing that, for those with connections.

Jesus says, '*All things* are possible, for those who believe'. Our sinful predilection for unbelief is not 'original sin' or a predetermined, permanent affliction. Our unbelief in the power of God is not 'the human condition'. Our unbelief is the carefully created, cultivated and orchestrated belief that the world is unchangeable, that human beings are dispensable, that justice is unattainable, that peace is impossible, that God is unable. And that is our real dilemma. And the people who make us believe that, make money by the bushel and continue to rule the world.

The challenge Jesus puts before this father is the challenge Jesus is putting before us: to believe that we can put ourselves at God's disposal and move mountains. To believe that God's ability to do can call forth our ability to believe. To have again a church so convicted of truth and justice, so firmly planted in faith, so relentlessly bent on making the world a living space for all God's creatures, on establishing justice so that '… every plant which my heavenly Father hath not planted shall be rooted up'. This is the kind of language of the early Calvinists that made an English writer say: 'I had rather see coming toward me a whole regiment with drawn swords, than one lone Calvinist convinced that he is doing the will of God'.

We don't have to be so frightening, but we do need faith. We do not need the old triumphalism, but we do need faith. We can do without the religious arrogance, but we do need faith. That faith that arises not from our self-assuredness, but from Jesus' help in overcoming our unbelief. That faith through which all things are possible.

Asking the Real Question

When the day of Pentecost had come, they were all
together in one place. And suddenly from heaven there
came the sound like the rush of a violent wind, and it filled
the entire house where they were sitting. Divided tongues,
as of fire, appeared among them, and a tongue rested on
each of them. All of them were filled with the Holy Spirit
and began to speak in other languages, as the Spirit gave
them ability. Now there were devout Jews from every
nation under heaven living in Jerusalem. And at this sound
the crowd gathered and was bewildered, because each one
heard them speaking in the native language of each. Amazed
and astonished, they asked, 'Are not all these who are
speaking Galileans? And how is it that we hear, each of us,
in our own native language? Parthians, Medes, Elamites, and
residents of Mesopotamia, Judea and Cappadocia, Pontus
and Asia, Phrygia and Pamphylia, Egypt and the parts of Libya
belonging to Cyrene, and visitors from Rome, both Jews
and Proselytes, Cretans and Arabs – in our own languages
we hear them speaking about God's deeds of power. All
were amazed and perplexed, saying to one another, 'What
does this mean?' But others sneered and said, 'They are filled
with new wine.' ... Therefore let the entire house of Israel
know with certainty that God has made him both Lord and
Messiah, this Jesus whom you crucified. Now when they
heard this, they were cut to the heart and said to Peter and
to the other apostles, 'Brothers, what should we do?'

Acts 2:1-13, 36-37

12

Isn't it just the truth? If one asks the wrong question, you're bound to get the wrong answer. To be sure, asking the right question may not always give us the answer we want, but it's sure to be the answer we need.

There is a marvellous story in the Hebrew Bible that illustrates this beautifully. We find that story in 1 Samuel chapter 4. The story begins with a shattering defeat for Israel on the battlefield. In the first clash against the Philistines Israel loses about four thousand men. Of course there are scholars who say that this is a typical hyperbole so often used in the Bible, but the number does want to indicate just how seriously the narrator wants us to take this story.

Now while Israel is thinking about this defeat, the question is raised, 'Why has the LORD brought defeat on us today before the Philistines?' It sounds like a good question. It even sounds a pious question. Israel does not say, 'Why are the Philistines so powerful that they can defeat us?' Or, 'Why do the Philistines have better weapons than we?' Or, 'Why do the Philistines have soldiers who are better trained than ours? Or perhaps, 'Are their generals better military strategists than ours?' No, none of that. Israel understands perfectly that it is not the Philistines, it is the LORD who is behind this. They know that they have to go to God with this.

But even if the question was a good question, it was not the right question. It did not go far enough. It was not radical enough. Israel should have known that for a loss of such a magnitude, something must have been radically wrong. So the question does not prompt the right answer. In response to that question they brought the ark into the camp. They thought that since the ark represents the presence of God, they could, like the Philistines, bring their God into the camp, into the battle, as it were. As long as we have God with us, they thought, things would go well. If God is with us, we cannot lose. But they did not think like the people of God. They thought like the Philistines. Yahweh cannot be manipulated, or commandeered, or controlled. Yahweh was waiting for another question; the right question.

Just one chapter before, we are told that things were far from well in Israel. 'The word of the LORD was rare in those days', the Bible says. Those ten words carry the full weight of the enormous calamity that cannot but befall Israel. Hophni and Phineas were 'priests before the LORD', but they made a mockery of the sacrifices, made prostitutes out of the women who served at the entrance of the Tabernacle, as if they were priestesses of Baal, and so 'despised' the LORD and treated Israel's God 'with contempt'. 'Thus the sin of the young men was very great in the sight of the LORD,' (1 Samuel 2:17) words that remind us of the gravity of the violence that caused the flood in Genesis 6, and of the sins of Sodom and Gomorrah in Genesis 19.

But Israel's pious, self-righteous question did not raise any of this. It missed the point. So bringing the ark into the camp did not help at all. Yahweh did not feel compelled to respond to Israel's manipulation. The earth might have resounded with the mighty shout of joy that rose from the Israelite camp when the ark arrived; the heavens, however, were silent:

> So the Philistines fought; Israel was defeated, and they
> fled, everyone to his home. There was a very great
> slaughter ... . (1 Samuel 4:10)

Sometimes one's very life depends on asking the right question.

II

The chapter we read together this morning begins with Luke's gripping account of the events on the day of Pentecost. There was the rush of wind, the tongues of fire, and the outpouring of the Holy Spirit. There were disciples who were Hebrews, but who spoke in every tongue represented in Jerusalem that day.

'Now there were devout Jews from every nation under heaven' (v. 5) does not simply mean that there were many languages spoken there. They were 'devout Jews', in other words things like miracles and wonders and signs were not alien to their thinking. They grew up with the stories of the plagues against Egypt, the splitting of the Red Sea, water from a rock and Elisha's axe that floated on the water. It means that what happened there that day was of such a magnitude, of such power, that *even they* were 'bewildered'.

And it is not just the wonder of the different tongues, it is the fact that they heard the disciples speak so that each, in their own language, could hear them speak, and could understand what they were saying. That is so often the problem of those Christians who think that 'speaking in tongues' is a special gift from God that makes one a 'better' Christian than others. It is, they proclaim, a 'blessing' that lifts one above others. It is a sign, they claim, that takes the Christian 'one step higher', 'one level up', out of the ordinary, makes one 'special'. They forget that what was said was said in perfectly understandable languages. That is why it made such an impression. It is a problem already Paul dealt with decisively in the first letter to the Corinthians, and it is superbly instructive that he makes a distinction between this speaking of tongues, which hopefully God understands, and prophecy, which is for the upbuilding and encouragement of others. Paul is clear: 'Those who speak in tongues build up themselves; those who prophesy build up the church' (1 Corinthians 14:4). We have to be especially careful: 'speaking in tongues' is often self-edification; prophecy is edification. The one serves the self, the other serves the church. The difference is not unimportant.

One other misunderstanding must be cleared up here. This text does not, as the apartheid theologians of the white Reformed Churches in South Africa used to say, express God's desire to separate the church on the basis of race, language and culture. The point here is not the *proliferation* of languages, but the fact that in all those different languages only one thing is spoken of: *the great deeds of God's power.* God liberating God's people from slavery, God sending the prophets to proclaim justice, God giving God's only begotten son, this Jesus, 'whom you have crucified' and whom God has made 'both Lord and Messiah'.

Then come the questions. 'Are not all these who are speaking Galileans?' 'How is it that we hear, each of us, in our own language?'

'What does this mean?' Not a single one of these questions is the right question; the Pentecost question. They do not reveal an honest desire to know, or to understand. They hide a human agenda: 'Are they not all from Galilee?'.

These people who gathered in Jerusalem for the feast, all came from afar, 'from every nation under heaven'. That means they could not have been poor. They must have had considerable wealth to make that long journey, to have had the time to take off, and to have enough for their sojourn in Jerusalem, to buy the sacrificial animals and pay the temple tax. That means that they were from the privileged classes, well-cushioned, educated people. No wonder they shared the disdain of so many of Galilee and its people. 'Can anything good come from Galilee?' was not just a local joke; it was an expression of class consciousness.

In Galilee they apparently did not speak proper Hebrew, or Aramaic. They spoke a kind of dialect some people find 'funny' or 'cute' and intellectuals think is 'quaint' or 'interesting', but not a proper language. That is what made this Pentecost phenomenon so intriguing. How can people who cannot even speak properly, poor, uneducated folk, all of a sudden speak in all the known languages of the world? And more pertinently, how can they presume to tell us what to do?

Most of those people from Galilee, a backward, rural area, were simple folk, with no real understanding of the complex social, political and theological issues of the day. Mostly they were artisans, workers like Joseph, the father of Jesus, or farmers, most of whom did not even own their own land, or fisher folk like those who followed Jesus. How many of them could afford the cost and the time for proper education? Were they trained in the exquisite nuances of the Torah and the Mishna by the Rabbis? What did they know about the mighty deeds of God? It is exactly the kind of question they asked about Jesus when he came to Nazareth. Don't we know his mother and father, his brothers and sisters? Who does he think he is – better than us? 'And they took offence at him,' the gospels tell us. They were not ready to be told about the great deeds of God by people who spoke township English.

It is something the church had to live with for a long time. 'Not many of you,' Paul had to comfort the Corinthians, 'were wise by human standards, not many were powerful, not many were of noble birth. But God chose what was foolish to shame the wise …' (1 Corinthians 1:26). They were mostly poor, mostly uneducated, mostly from the lower classes, many were slaves, and since joining the church, they were suspect, marginalised, setting themselves up against society's rules, expectations and mores. They chose against the Caesar and for Christ, against the powerful and for the powerless. They chose for the God who resurrected Jesus, against the gods of the empire who executed Jesus. In a word, Paul said, they were foolish. It all began on that Pentecost day.

The church hears that often today. 'What do you know about politics?' we are asked. Or about the subtle workings of the economy? What do you understand about the complexities of political power, the sensitivities of the market, the difficulties of globalisation, or the intricacies of the law? Why don't you leave all that to the experts? And yes, mostly the church did leave all that to the experts – and look at the mess we are all in now!

The church might not be what the world calls 'expert', but it knows about justice. It might not be expert, but it knows what the LORD requires: to do justice, to love mercy, and to walk humbly with God. It might not be expert, but it knows the God who lifts up the poor from the dust of the earth, who breaks the bow of the mighty and the powerful, who teaches us that not by might shall one prevail. It may not be expert, but it knows that to do justice and righteousness, to judge the cause of the poor and the needy, is to know the LORD. It might not be expert, but it knows: without the love of God, the world shall perish. It might not be expert, but it understands that without the compassionate politics of Jesus, our politics is no more than calculated, secular casuistry.

III

No, none of these questions is the real question; the Pentecost question. And because it is not the right question, the answer is wrong: '… They are full of sweet wine.'(v.13) That's right. You want justice for the poor? You talk of clothing the naked, feeding the hungry? You want to challenge the powerful and protect the weak and defenceless? You want to talk about peace as if you believe in it? You want to stop war? You believe that stopping an Iraqi child from dying in war is as important as saving a South African child from hunger? You speak of giving those with AIDS their life back? You are convinced that to stop a person from remaining a criminal they need more than just a job – they also need Jesus in their lives? You believe that the scourge of poverty cannot just be alleviated, it can actually be *eradicated*? Really? You must be drunk. Don't you know how the real world works? You must be crazy! You must be a disciple of *that Man*.

It should drive us to drink that nobody accuses the church of being full of sweet wine any more.

But the real question gets asked only after Peter has spoken. What did he say? He told them that Pentecost was the fulfilment of God's promises.

> In the last days it will be, says the LORD, that I will
> pour out my Spirit on all flesh; and your sons and your
> daughters shall prophesy and your young men shall see
> visions and your old men shall dream dreams. On **both**
> men and women I will pour out my Spirit and they shall
> prophesy … . Then **everyone** who calls on the name of
> the LORD shall be saved.
> (Joel 2:28, 29, 32)

Israel had never allowed the full power and radicality of this text to impact its life. The Christian church did, in the beginning, following the example set by Jesus. But by the time the person who wrote in Paul's name told the church that, in every place, he desires that 'the men should pray', while women should only 'dress modestly and decently in suitable clothing', learning 'in silence with full submission', never to be 'permitted' to teach or have authority over a man, but 'to keep silent' (1 Timothy 2:8-12), the church too, had forgotten this text and its beginnings. The church had by then submitted to the sinful pressures of the men, bowed down to the demands of the dominant culture, set aside the word of the prophet, spurned the meaning of Pentecost, denied its Lord.

The alienation from God must have run deep in the church to have accepted as gospel those inexplicable words that a woman 'will be saved through childbearing, provided they [her children?] continue in faith and love and holiness, with modesty' (1 Timothy 2:15). Here there is no sign that women were given their rightful place by Jesus; that the prophet Joel was so emphatic about God's inclusion of both men and women in the outpouring of the Holy Spirit, or even that women, as men, are saved through faith in Jesus Christ. The alienation must have been as severe as was the alienation in Israel when Eli, Hophni and Phineas were priests, when the Word of the LORD was scarce, and when the people of Israel could not find enough truth in themselves to ask the right questions. Just as, apparently, the right questions about women in the church were not asked at that time.

We, however, must ask those questions. What happened to the Paul who was 'not ashamed of the gospel, for it is the power of God for salvation to *everyone who has faith* ...' (Romans 1:16); the man who was so convinced that the righteous shall live by faith alone (Romans 1:17)? Where is the man who sent greetings to a woman called Junia, calling her 'prominent among the apostles' (Romans 16:7)? Where is the church that witnessed the outpouring of the Holy Spirit on *all* who were present on that day? Where is the church who welcomed bright and gifted young men like Apollos, already 'well-versed in the Scriptures', and who spoke 'with burning enthusiasm and taught accurately' about the things concerning Jesus, yet needed to be taught by a woman named Priscilla 'even more accurately' the Way of God (Acts 18:24-28)? No, something went radically wrong with us. We have lost the way, and we must find it, or we shall wither and die.

Pentecost means the radical inclusion of all who call upon the name of the LORD. No longer just a small, select group, a chosen few. They are called regardless of status or sex or station in life.

Not just the eloquent, the gifted or the educated, but *all flesh*. Not just the young and the strong. Not just the men, *all flesh*. Not just heterosexual men and women, all flesh. The day Joel could not wait for, the day when all those men and women stood in astonishment to listen to Peter – that is the day Moses longed for:

> Oh, would that all the LORD's people were prophets,
> and that the LORD would pour his Spirit upon them!
> (Numbers 11:29)

This has happened. This is the meaning of Pentecost. And so this Peter, who could not acknowledge Jesus in the courtyard of the High Priest not so long ago, found his voice and spoke with such boldness that all who listened to him were 'cut to the heart'.

IV

What did they hear? First of all, they were told 'of the great deeds of God's power' by everyone on whom the Spirit descended. Then Peter tells them about Joel's prophecy being fulfilled on Pentecost. To all those devout Jews the implications must have been crystal clear. Peter speaks of Jesus, his deeds of power, his life and his death at the hands of those 'outside the law'. He speaks of Jesus' resurrection from the dead, because 'it was impossible for him to be held in [death's] power'. This Spirit, Peter says, whom they have seen at work that day, comes from this exalted Jesus. He has been rejected, accused, denied, betrayed, killed. But now they must know 'with certainty that God has made him both Lord and Messiah …'.

Now, only now, do they ask the real question: 'Brothers, what should we do?' Now they understood. But they understood only when a Spirit-filled church is ready to testify that Jesus is Lord. The world will only learn to ask the real question if the church today speaks like the church on Pentecost.

We must tell the world that thinks it can live without him that Jesus is Lord. We must tell those who claim his name to justify a fascist Christian political agenda: Jesus is Lord. We must tell the powerful, who think that they are gods unto themselves, that Jesus is Lord.

We must remind the church which lives so comfortably with its own sins that the Spirit of the LORD has fallen upon all who call upon God's name, and that no one, *no one* has the right to exclude those whom God has called. We must tell them until they learn to ask the right question, so that they know what to do. For the promise of Pentecost is 'for you, for your children, and for all who are far away, *everyone whom the Lord our God calls to him'*. Learning to ask the right question, the Pentecost question, may just give the church back her life, and her testimony.

The Heart of the Matter

If I speak in the tongues of mortals and of angels,
but do not have love, I am a noisy gong or a clanging
cymbal. And if I have prophetic powers, and understand
all mysteries and all knowledge, and if I have all faith
so as to move mountains, but do not have love, I am
nothing. If I give away all my possessions, and if I hand
over my body to be burned, but do not have love, I
gain nothing. Love is patient; love is kind; love is not
envious or boastful or rude. It does not insist on its own
way; it is not irritable or resentful; it does not rejoice in
wrongdoing, but rejoices in the truth. It bears all things,
hopes all things, endures all things. Love never ends.
But as for prophecies, they will come to an end; as for
tongues, they will cease; as for knowledge, it will come
to an end. For we know only in part; and we prophesy
in part; but when the complete comes, the partial will
come to an end. When I was a child, I spoke like a
child, I thought like a child, I reasoned like a child; when
I became an adult, I put an end to childish ways. For
now we see in a mirror dimly, but then we will see face
to face. Now I only know in part; then I will know fully,
even as I have been fully known. And now faith, hope
and love abide, these three; and the greatest of these is
love.

I Corinthians 13:1-13

13

I

Those of us fortunate enough to have travelled abroad, must have noticed that in those countries where English is not the native language, some restaurants and shops have the helpful habit putting a sign in the window, saying, 'English Spoken Here'. That is not only helpful, it makes good business sense. A visitor from abroad knows immediately: here is a place where I can feel at home. No worries about whether I will be understood, or whether I might make a fool of myself trying to bargain or order in English while people stare at me like I come from Mars. No stumbling, fumbling or mumbling or casting your eyes to the heavens for help when you need to find that perfect souvenir. No needless stress about the pronunciation of those tongue twisters you have endlessly practised in front of the mirror, but are sure to completely forget the moment a German shop assistant says, 'Ja bitte?' It is also immensely comforting, and believe me, it makes a great deal of difference whether one enjoys one's trip abroad or not. Walking down a foreign shopping street, that's the place you will choose.

I sometimes feel that Christian churches should have a sign on the front door: 'Love Spoken Here'. Don't you think that is a great idea? For is that not what we are all about, after all is said and done? People who look for comfort, or joy, or salvation or hope will know immediately: this is the place. This is it. So since today's sermon is about the nature of the Christian church, it is about the foolishness of love. Yes, you heard right: not just about love, but about the *foolishness* of love.

The first letter to the Corinthians is Paul's most comprehensive attempt to explain the nature of the Christian church. In painstaking detail, with infinite patience, he speaks of what it means to be the church of Jesus Christ. The issues involved here are not theoretical. Paul is not writing an ecclesiological treatise: he addresses the problems and questions as they are encountered in the life of the church. The church's firm foundation is not numerical strength or worldly power, but the grace of God and the peace of the Lord Jesus Christ. The bedrock of the church is not the approval of society or the blessing of the dominant culture, but 'the name of Jesus Christ' (1:2). The strength of the church lies not in any guarantees given by Caesar, but in the faithfulness of God (1:9).

Paul wastes no time to make clear what belongs to the essence of the church. He prays that the church will be united 'in the same mind and the same purpose' (1:10), a theme he emphasises again and again. 'Has Christ been divided?' (1:13); 'What then is Apollos? What is Paul?' (3:5), but 'God's servants, working together' (3:9). The church is not of Paul, or Cephas, or Apollos, but its foundation is Jesus Christ (3:11). The church has many members, but is one body, 'for in the one Spirit we were all baptized into one body – Jews or Greeks, slaves or free ...' (11:13).

The church is called to proclaim Christ crucified, but it is warned that this will be regarded as 'foolishness' (1:18); however, it is God's wisdom and God's power, and the church ought to remember that the foolishness of God 'is wiser than human wisdom' (1:25). Repeatedly Paul warns that the church should not be seduced by what the world regards as wisdom, for the wisdom of the world is foolishness with God. (3:1) We must be ready to follow the example of Christ, and be fools for Christ, ready to endure hunger and thirst, to be beaten and homeless, reviled, persecuted, slandered, and in response not to seek vengeance since we cannot expect justice, but instead to bless, endure, speak kindly. To be church, we must be ready to be regarded as 'the rubbish of the world, the dregs of all things' (4:12, 13).

Indeed, this is not a neat ecclesiology in which the church is known by its orthodoxy, but rather by its life, the authenticity of its witness, its willingness to suffer for the sake of Christ. It is not so much the correctness of dogma that marks the church here, as it is its obedience to Jesus Christ.

In chapter 12 Paul returns to what he obviously regards as essential: the unity of the body of Christ. The diversity of gifts he dwells upon is not to emphasizse the disunity of the church, but rather to proclaim the glory of the one Giver of gifts, 'one and the same Spirit'. 'The same Spirit' he says over and over again. The same Spirit gives different gifts, different kinds of working, but it is the 'same God' who works in all of us. All the great gifts, 'the message of wisdom', 'the message of knowledge', 'the faith', the 'gift of healing', the gift of 'miraculous powers' or prophecy, or the distinguishing of spirits, or the speaking of different kinds of tongues and the interpretation of it – 'all these are the work of one and the same Spirit ...' (12:7-11). And the one Spirit does the one work in the whole church, to the body 'as a unit', as one body. 'For we were al baptized in one Spirit into one body – whether Jews or Greeks, slave or free, and we were all given the one Spirit to drink' (v.13). It cannot be stressed enough: one Giver of gifts, one baptism, one Spirit, one body.

To be sure, the argument with which Paul follows the above in chapter 12, namely that we are all different parts of the one body, some are like the foot, others like the hand, the eye, the ear and so forth, had been used before. When the peasants threatened revolt against the aristocracy of the Roman Empire, the aristocrat Menelaus Agrippa convinced them that although they were less noticeable members, they were nonetheless necessary, and had a role to play just like the upper classes. Different and separate, but equal. This piece of sophistry was an attempt to fool the masses and to keep them down, to quell any resistance to the existing structures of oppression and discrimination. Marvellous actually, how Paul could use this same style of argument and turn it upside down. For him, the point of departure is not the 'separate but equal' philosophy, which in practice merely confirmed the inequalities in the Empire and the abuse of the trust of the people by the aristocracy. His point of departure is that the church, in its oneness, and in its different gifts, are the body of Christ, the temple of God, in whom the Spirit of God dwells! In the temple everything is sacred, the temple as a whole is God's claimed place, the temple as a whole is sanctified by God's presence. And *all* shall bow down to acknowledge this presence. Hence, in another place, Paul's admonition, 'Submit *to one another* ...' (Ephesians 5:21). And this, again (!), is said within the context of the unity of the body, which begins with living a life worthy of the calling they have received.

Make every effort to keep the unity of the Spirit
through the bond of peace … There is one body and
one Spirit – just as you were called to one hope when
you were called – one Lord, one faith, one baptism; one
God and Father of all, who is over all and through all,
and in all. (Ephesians 4:1-6)

So there is no patronising condescension here, tricking the restless in the church into submission. Paul is not into clever politicking. It is celebrating the gracious gifts of God who through the one work of the one Spirit equips the church for our ministry in the world. But Paul does something else here too. First, he emphasises the unity of the church, and then, most importantly, tries to show 'the more excellent way'.

We sometimes forget just what a battle is has been to come to this understanding, how hard it was, and how long it took. The book of Acts is a record of the struggle of the church to be the church. They were still glowing from the holy fire when Ananias and Sapphira, and with them the whole church, had to learn the cost of breaking the law of love (5:1-11). Even after the dramatic scene in which Philip baptizes the Ethiopian court official, demonstrating the openness (and the oneness!) of the Christian church (8:26-40), Peter first has to be convinced by God through a vision before understanding that God is opening wide the doors of the church so that Cornelius and all who were with him could come into 'the presence of God to listen to all that the Lord has commanded you to say' (10:33).

Acts chapter 9 is not only the account of Paul's conversion, but an account also of how difficult it was for the church to accept him, to believe him, to trust him, to include him; in other words, to love him. Paul, a repentant persecutor and murderer, now called by God, confronted by the risen Christ, must be welcome in the church. Paul, the man who used to 'breathe threats and murder' against the fledgling church, the man who sought letters of authority from the High Priest to seek out, hunt down, 'any who belonged to the Way, men or women', and bring them 'bound' to Jerusalem. The murderous zealot who 'approved' of the killing of Stephen. This man must now be welcomed in the church and called 'brother'. How hard it is! First for Ananias (vv.13, 14), but also for the disciples (v.26). If it were not for the courage of the gentle Barnabas …

With how much vigour and conviction, and with how much pain did Paul have to confront Peter in Antioch when Peter refused to eat with Gentiles? Paul's rebuke of Peter was severe, for Peter was making others 'join his hypocrisy', keeping himself 'separate', 'not acting consistently with the gospel'. Not to eat with Gentile brothers and sisters, is to refuse to love them. And in withholding his love Peter was shunning Christ. This we read not in Acts, but in Galatians 2. To understand what it means to be the church, to witness to the truth of the gospel, to live, not for oneself, but for Christ, to see the unity of the church as obedience to the prayers of Jesus, to love without reservation, to be fools for Christ, to succumb to a love that supersedes culture and race, and class, and privilege, that is what it means to be church of Jesus Christ, to be 'crucified with Christ'.

Yet we sometimes act as if none of this has any meaning at all. We split the church on the basis of race, class, politics, ethnicity and sexuality. Our own history of racism in the church in this country, in Afrikaans and English language churches alike, remains a painful example of how easily this can happen, and how tenacious it can be. Far too often in the church a person's skin colour is more important than that person's faith; a person's class is more important than whether that person believes; we are more worried about whether a person is gay or lesbian than whether that person shares our faith in Jesus Christ. We are far more sensitive to the voice of blood and kinship, of culture and race; of money; status and power than to the voice of the gospel. We have completely forgotten what it means to be the church of Jesus Christ. We are all one in Christ, and we understand that truly only when we understand what Paul calls 'the more excellent way'.

II

Paul uses an entire chapter just to make this point. The 'more excellent way' comes as the culmination of all that Paul has mentioned thus far: wisdom, unity, spiritual gifts, caring and solidarity, understanding the meaning of the table of the Lord. All of this receives meaning when we understand the essence of it all: love. And then Paul launches into a celebration of love that stands as one of the most amazing pieces of literature in the Bible, or anywhere, for that matter. For Christians in our postmodern world it is somewhat surprising, somewhat embarrassing. We hear the word 'love' and we think immediately of sentimentality, of romance, of what is called 'matters of the heart'. We fear, with some trepidation, that Paul is getting mushy on us, to manipulate us with emotion. It is not about matters of the heart, but about the heart of the matter.

Talk of love gives us a feeling of helplessness, and that is not fair. It replaces reason and logic, suspends clear-headed thinking. Or so we think. It demands that we live as if we were not in the real world. Or so we think. Is that perhaps why we have removed 1 Corinthians 13 from the category of 'church' and placed it in the category of 'wedding texts', along with the book of Ruth? That way, most of us have to deal with it only once or twice in our lives. At some deep level, we suspect that it wants to rob us of our adulthood. I don't exactly know how to put this. The Germanic languages have a word for it: *Mundigkeit*, the Germans call it. Not only us as individuals, but the human race as a whole have come of age. We have seen too much, experienced too much, heard too much, been hoodwinked and lied to too often. The twentieth century has been a steep learning curve, and it has made us cynical of life, wary of each other, suspicious of God. In the movie, *The Devil's Advocate*, Al Pacino, as the Devil, exclaims triumphantly, 'Let's face it: the twentieth century was indisputably mine!' We suspect that he is right and we want to deal with that on our own terms. And in our terms, love was the Devil's first victim because it is our greatest weakness. We do not want to be treated like children who don't know better, and who cannot see the woods for the butterflies.

But that is exactly what love does not do, Paul argues. Learning to love is precisely 'to put an end to childish ways'! To love is to know and to have true wisdom, to speak words of truth. Not being able to love is to speak like a child, think like a child, reason like a child. What we think of as foolish childishness: to be patient, kind, not envious or boastful or arrogant; not to insist on our own ways, not to be irritable or rude or resentful; not to rejoice in evil but to rejoice with the truth: now that, Paul says, is the hallmark of adulthood, of genuine humanbeingness, But this goes against the grain. It is the complete reversal of our way of thinking and living. It is a condemnation of our history, a judgement on what we think of as our values, a fundamental challenge to our notions of what makes a person or a people great.

To make it in this world, we think, is to be the opposite of what Paul is speaking of. Come on, let's get real here! Patience blunts our ambition; kindness is for wimps, envy spurs us on to do better, is in fact the perfect driving force in today's competitive working atmosphere. Boastfulness is so much part of our culture we hardly recognise it when we see it, and what would politicians do without it? Arrogance is simply good defence strategy. Resentment gives us an edge, aggression gives us first-strike ability and showing all that anger is good for the self-image, we are told by the popular psychologists on TV. Not insisting on our own way means people walk all over you and rudeness is its own reward. Nothing sums it up better that that wonderful American phrase, 'Nice guys finish last!' It is not for nothing that military terms have become such an essential part of our ordinary discourse.

Paul knows how our minds work. That is why he takes so much time at the beginning of this letter to speak about the wisdom of the world which is exposed as foolishness by the wisdom of God. The world sees the cross, giving one's life for others as foolishness. But for those who believe, it is the power of God. It is the power that shames the strong, that reduces to nothing the things that are. This is the love Paul is talking about, that we must make our own. This is the love that confronts evil and rejoices with the truth. This is the love that gives us, weak as we think we are, battle-hardened as we believe ourselves to be, the strength to endure, even if the road is long and the battle is hard. Not having this love is the epitome of foolishness, the height of childishness. It is to surrender our adulthood, that maturity which comes from understanding the wisdom of God.

III

This love, like all else Paul speaks of, is a gift from God. It is the love of God. It is God's commitment to the restoration, recreation, resurrection of God's world and God's people. It is God's determination not to give up on us, not to despair of us.

When God loves, the chaos, formlessness and darkness disappear; then there is light before the sun and moon and stars are made; then there is heaven and earth, beasts in the field, birds in the sky, and human beings, created in the image and likeness of God.

When God loves, God's everlasting commitment to life is caught up in the brilliant colours of a rainbow that spans the heavens. Then a promise is made to Abraham, Sarah and Isaac, to Hagar and Ishmael and in them to all who believe and dare to press God on these promises.

When God loves, Egypt is overcome, the might of the Pharaoh is challenged, the chains of slavery are broken; the sea is split in two, God's people walk through and live, not only to see the Egyptians dead on the sea shore, but they live to sing the song of Moses:

> I will sing to the LORD, for he has triumphed gloriously;
> Horse and rider he has thrown into the sea.
> The LORD is my strength and my might,
> And he has become my salvation.
> (Exodus 5:1, 2)

When God loves, there is a cloud by day and a pillar of fire by night, manna from heaven and sweet water from the rock. Then Jordan, that mighty river, becomes just one more river to cross; then the walls of Jericho come tumbling down.

When God loves, God's faithfulness fills the void in Hannah's life and her song merges with the song of Mary, next to which every revolutionary song since then pales into insignificance. Then the bow of the mighty is broken, the hungry are filled with good things, the proud are scattered in the thoughts of their hearts, and the powerful are brought down from their thrones.

When God loves, the barriers are broken down, the poor hear the good news, women are given their rightful place, centre stage with Jesus instead of in the margins; sins are forgiven, the blind see and the lame walk; prisoners are set free and the spirit of the Lord comes down. Then the dumb become prophets, the old dream dreams and the young see visions. Then the weak gird on strength and learn to speak and act with boldness.

When God loves, the cross, sign of shame and condemnation, becomes a sign of salvation. The cross, sign of weakness, becomes a sign of the power of God. Then a stone is rolled away and the power of death is broken. When God loves, hell is shamed into silence, and Satan falls like lightning from heaven.

When God loves, the church is given life, ordinary people speak and act with extraordinary courage, the downtrodden walk with dignity, evil is confronted and conquered. Then the hungry are fed, the naked are clothed and the poor receive justice. Women become the first messengers of the message of the resurrection, and no one is excluded from the church of Christ.

Then, once powerful empires, to the utter astonishment of the world, grind to a halt in their deluded march to immortality; then the Berlin wall falls, apartheid crumbles to dust, the truth is heard and seen, every idol quakes on its feet of clay, and like Dagon, falls on its face in the glorious presence of the Holy One.

Our love, that love that Paul urges us to embrace, is a response to this love of God. It is not some vague, sentimental emotion, some feeble romantic feeling. To love thus, is to explore the open spaces beyond our own limitations, to surrender to the power of our wider imagining. To discover in the other the best that we ourselves want to be, to offer to the other more than we, in our self-induced timidity,

CHAPTER 13

have allowed ourselves to be.

To love thus is to make choices: for rejoicing in the truth rather than to profit from evil. To expose the foolishness of the world by allowing ourselves to be claimed and edified by the wisdom of God. To shame the wisdom of the world by becoming fools for Christ. To spurn the wisdom of the world and choose for justice, peace and genuine reconciliation. To seek our strength in the imitation of Christ and to resist emulating the world. To seek to do what is right, rather than what is popular. To find, in the defencelessness of the cross the strength to love, to stand up for the poor and the needy, the excluded and the marginalised.

IV

The first words of 1 Corinthians 13 sound like hammer blows on rock, and they echo with a power that causes us to tremble. 'If I … .' Five times, 'If I … .' And these are not just frivolous things Paul is mentioning, mind you. To speak in the tongues of mortals and angels, to have prophetic powers and understand all mysteries and all knowledge; to have the faith to move mountains, just as Jesus had promised; to have the selflessness that knows the true value of possessions; and oh, to have the courage to be willing to sacrifice my life when that is called for. To have all that is to have discovered the true meaning of life. How have Christians over the ages tortured themselves, flagellated and humiliated themselves in vain efforts to attain what Paul throws aside as worthless if we have not love.

For without love all this is futile, nothing, vain. Three times Paul says it: I am a noisy gong, I am nothing, I gain nothing. For without love we lack the patience that allows wisdom to mature; we miss the kindness which is the mirror of God's mercy; we are the slaves of envy and greed, our boastfulness is a trap of our own making and our arrogance is a constant temptation to play God. Without love we will never know the joys of human relationships, or the healing of forgiveness and true reconciliation. Without love we know only the perverted pleasures of evil and we will never know what it means to join the truth in the feast of justice. Without love, we do not have the strength to bear the burdens of life, to fight the cynicism which chokes us to death, to endure the pain and enlighten the times of darkness. Without love we are adrift, alone on a restless sea of hopelessness and despair. In short, our life is nothing.

The meaning of human existence, the quality of human life, is measured by our capacity to love. This is the love that never fails. It is stronger than its enemies, outlives hatred and enmity, soars above arrogance, is stronger than death. It remains, a pulsing, joyful reality, when all other things have ceased to exist. Its resilience outlasts the litany of cessation Paul intones over prophecies, tongues and knowledge: they will come to an end ... they will cease ... they will come to an end. Love, only love, remains.

It is a lesson we must heed, and yet are loath to learn. Our foolishness calls this wisdom foolish. But we must heed this love Paul speaks of. In a world of calculated cynicism, of cold-blooded treachery and incipient corruption, of deliberate deception and appalling indifference, we need it. In a world of endless deception, with integrity and trust crucified, we need this love.

Oh, I know: we resist and resent it. Its presence offends us, its demands appall us. Confronted with love, we balk. And so, Mahatma Ghandi dies at an assassin's hand. Martin Luther King Jr. is murdered. Steve Biko is tortured to death. And what more should we say, except to say it with the writer of the letter to the Hebrews,

> Others suffered mocking and flogging, and even chains
> and imprisonment. They were stoned to death, they
> were sawn in two, they were killed by the sword; they
> went about in skins of sheep and goats, destitute,
> persecuted, tormented – the world was not worthy of
> them .... (11:37, 38)

V

'And now faith, hope and love abide ... .' We always think the chapter ends here. It does not. It ends with chapter 14:1: 'Pursue love ...'. That is Paul's last word on the subject. Pursue it, take hold

---

of it, own it, hold on to it, love it, live it!

If we don't, humanity stands no chance. If we don't, there is nothing between us and the barbarism of lovelessness. If we don't, there will be no justice, only legalism. Truth will remain crushed to earth, and the lie will wear the cloak of righteousness. If we don't, power will remain heartless, and powerlessness will be sanctified. If we don't, our hope remains vacuous, our faith becomes sterile dogma and we ourselves fruitless trees. If we don't, we will not know how to respond to the love of God. If we don't, we will not know how to be the church of Jesus Christ in the world. And that, beloved, is the heart of the matter.

The Three-Mile-an-Hour God

This is now, beloved, the second letter I am writing
to you; in them I am trying to arouse your sincere
intention by reminding you that you should remember
the words spoken in the past by the holy prophets, and
the commandment of the Lord and Saviour spoken
through your apostles. First of all you must understand
this, that in the last days scoffers will come, scoffing
and indulging their own lusts and saying, 'Where is the
promise of his coming? For ever since our ancestors
died all things continue as they were from the beginning
of creation!' They deliberately ignore this fact, that by
the word of God heavens existed long ago and an
earth was formed out of water and by means of water,
through which the world of that time was deluged with
water and perished. But by the same word the present
heavens and earth have been reserved for fire, being
kept until the day of judgement and the destruction of
the godless. But do not ignore this one fact, beloved,
that with the Lord one day is like a thousand years,
and a thousand years are like one day. The Lord is not
slow about his promise, as some think of slowness, but
is patient with you, not wanting any to perish, but all to
come to repentance.

2 Peter 3:1-8

14

I

In our best moments, the Christian church, we hope, is characterised by hope, faith and love. And a bit of courage might do nicely as well. But mostly these days, if we care to be honest, it is bewilderment, confusion and weariness. It is not so much sinful as dispiriting. We wonder why we have so little impact on the world, why the days of 'church influence' on society have passed so quickly, and why our voice has become so insignificant, hardly heard. At a deeper level, we worry why justice is so hard and peace so seemingly unattainable.

The bullies still run the world, the powerful still run amok with impunity. They seem to have become a permanent fixture: the bullies of Iraq are replaced by the bullies from Washington and London and the weak and defenceless continue to suffer. The inheritance of the meek is scorched earth, polluted rivers and poisoned seas, denuded forests and tin and cardboard shacks among stinking, toxic dumps they must call 'home'. We reel from shock as the statistics of women and child abuse in this country are made public and we are stunned into silence by the indifference of men on this issue, even some in high office.

The world remains depressingly unchanged, and we seem to be fighting the same battles over and over again. And it is not for want of trying: it's just that the resistance is so great, that power is so corrupt and perpetually corrupting, that quiescence is so easy, that fellow Christians are so complacent, so in love with compromise, so happy with their own comfort, so undisturbed at the fact that we are so disturbed. When is God going to change all of this? Why is God sitting around, twiddling his thumbs? Why are we burning with impatience while God seems to have all the time in the world?

What kind of God is this, is the question that burns up our hearts. Why does God move so slowly through history? God is, as captured in the title of a well-known book by my friend and colleague, Kosuke Koyama, a 'three-mile-an-hour God'. God has all the time in the world while we who are in the world, feel that we have no time at all.

Well, we are not the first to feel this way. The Christians in Peter's congregation were asking the same thing. Why does everything remain the same? Why has nothing changed? They found it incomprehensible. They were a small minority, this Christian community, pitted against the inflexibility of the Synagogue and the merciless power of Rome. They were third-class citizens, the suspect members of a new and thoroughly unwelcome sect that had caused much trouble to Romans and the Jewish establishment.

Mostly poor, (not many of noble birth, Paul would say of them), mostly slaves, in many places mostly women, different from the rest of society and therefore considered deviant and dangerous. They cannot call the Emperor 'god'; refuse to do military service, engaging in foolish talk such as 'love your enemies', 'bless those who abuse you', and 'turn the other cheek'. Their loyalty is not to country, or people, or the emperor, but to the one they call 'Lord'. Already this has caused them much suffering and abuse. Peter tells them to 'endure', for if they suffer for doing justice they must count that a blessing (1 Peter 3). They are going through a 'fiery ordeal' (1 Peter 4:12), and are reviled 'for the name of Christ' (4:14). Peter advises:

> Therefore, let those suffering in accordance with God's
> will entrust themselves to a faithful Creator, while
> continuing to do good. (4:19)

But that advice, good as it might sound, can take one only so far. The longing bursts from the heart: if only Christ could come in all his glory, sweep away the ungodly and establish his reign upon the earth! After all, is that not what he has promised? Is that not what happened in days of Noah and the flood? Is such a cleansing not the indisputable answer to the problem? So why is God so excruciatingly slow? Why allow all this suffering to go on and on? We are in pain, Peter's church is saying, and we cannot wait – not for one day or one hour. To allow the suffering is to delay the promise. To make us wait is to extend the pain. If the Caesar cannot go – let Christ come! God's tardiness is, let's face it, a betrayal of the promise. God has betrayed us – God has betrayed God.

The prophets could still speak of a hidden God. But in Jesus God has been revealed. We have seen God in what Jesus had done in this world for the weak, the poor and the needy, the dejected and despised. 'Who has seen me,' said Jesus, 'has seen the Father.' In other words, who has seen me act, has seen the father act. God's power, God's love and mercy, God's compassionate justice, have come to life in the words and deeds of Jesus of Nazareth.

But Jesus has disappeared behind the clouds, the ancestors who have been with him and who were witnesses of those mighty deeds, have died or are no longer immediately among them. The eyewitnesses who have seen and heard him are gone. The second generation, experiencing rejection from the synagogue, alienation from their roots, and terror from Rome, must ask, 'Where is the promise of his coming?'.

II

The question comes from two quarters, first from the 'scoffers' (vv. 3, 4). They are those who, as in Psalm 42, look at the world, the pain of the weak and the suffering of the just, and ask, mockingly, 'Where is your God?'. Peter has no truck with them. Their desire for 'the promise of his coming' is not the longing for that moment that 'every knee shall bow and every tongue confess him Lord'. Rather, it is a reproach to a God who keeps on deferring judgement, a longing for the God of the flood 'through which the world of that time was deluged with water and perished'. They cannot wait for the fire reserved for the day of judgement, because their faith in Jesus rests upon the 'destruction of the godless'. God must 'prove' himself, and in proving himself, must vindicate them.

It is this vengeful sinfulness, posing as holy impatience that Peter exposes. They are driven, not by love for the Lord or by a longing for the salvation of the world, but by the indulgence of their 'lusts'. It is not the coming of the Lord, but the *judgement* of the Lord that inspires them. Not the salvation of the world, but the destruction of the wicked will be their vindication. They have forgotten who God is:

> For I have no pleasure in the death of anyone, says the
> LORD GOD. Repent and live. (Ezekial 18:32)

Repentance, conversion, forgiveness, transformation – that is what will hasten the coming of the Lord, not God's desire for punishment and death.

In verse 8, however, Peter's tone is entirely different. 'Beloved', he calls them. These are not the scoffers, but those believers who have been brought to doubt by the scoffers of vv. 3 and 4. The pain of the world is their pain, their suffering for 'doing what is right' is acute, and their efforts seem in vain. Their cry for 'the promise of his coming' comes from a very different heart.

Christians who believe in, and try to work for justice know that well. We are often brought to doubt and near despair when our work seems to make no impression. The people who point to the growing numbers of AIDS victims, to too many children still dying of hunger; to poor peasants driven off their land to make room for 'development' which brings more money to multinational companies; to the scattered remains of children blown up by landmines, or to the appalling indifference of so many in the church, ask: 'Where is your God?'.

And we have nowhere to run. Not into the world, for there lies our guilt, and not to heaven, for there lies our problem. We have nothing to say, except, 'Where is the promise of his coming?'. And so, those who mock our faith make us doubt our faith.

To those, to us, Peter says, 'beloved'. And is that not immensely comforting? For the doubters are not cast out, they belong within the family. And, honestly speaking, are we not *both*, believers *and* doubters? Do we not pray often because we doubt? And do we not often doubt *because* we pray? And do we not doubt *in spite* of our prayers? Since Jeremiah we can believe that God does not love us because we never doubt God's word, because we are always sturdy of faith and strong of heart. Jeremiah speaks for all of us:

> O LORD you have enticed (misled) me, and I was
> enticed .... (20:7)

---

and,

> Cursed be the day on which I was born! The day when
> my mother bore me, let it not be blessed! Cursed be
> the man who brought the news to my father, saying,
> 'A child is born to you, a son,' making him very glad ...
> (20:14, 15)

and even stronger,

> Truly, you are to me like a deceitful brook, like waters
> that fail ... (15:18).

Jeremiah's faith drives him to doubt and his doubt drives him to God. And he is not the only one. We must not be afraid to acknowledge it, and we must not fear that our wrestling with God's promises is a sign of unfaithfulness. 'Beloved doubters' – Peter knows all about it. His own denial of Jesus was not the result of his fear, but of his impatience. A Messiah who tarries too long is no Messiah.

III

So Peter responds: 'One thing you must not forget, beloved, that with the Lord one day is like a thousand years, and a thousand years are like one day ...'.

But how does that help us? It's alright if you are God and time does not matter, but what about us? We don't live that long, we can't really deal with that. So we tried to make sense of it:

First we said, it is God's punishment, all the suffering we see and experience. But we really could not persist: a deformed baby, or a child that dies of leukemia – God's punishment?

Then we said it is 'divine pedagogy', in the same way the Reformers defined one of the ways God uses the Ten Commandments: the *usus paedagogicus*. God wants to teach us something. God wants to teach us *life*. But what lessons do we really learn from living with centuries of pain and suffering? Is the remedy not much worse than the ailment?

Finally, we said, God does not want this. It is people who are doing it. I believe this might indeed be closer to the truth, but it does not answer all the questions: if people are doing all this evil, is God then powerless to stop them? The world is already full of wonderful, but powerless people. What do we do with a powerless God?

But we have to take this text seriously. Peter's response does not end with the reminder of God's 'thousand years'. The Lord is not slow, says Peter, God does not unnecessarily delay, 'but is patient with you.' The delay of the promise is connected in the first place, not to the unpreparedness of the world, but to the unreadyness of the 'beloved'. In other words, God is waiting on us, on our conversion.

Doing justice in the world is our calling; loving one another is our responsibility; feeding the hungry, clothing the naked, stopping war, the glorification of violence and senseless killing, is *our* responsibility. Protecting the weak, aiding the needy, creating communities of love, justice and compassion, is *our* responsibility. Challenging the loveless powers with God's truth is our calling. Calling the world to repentance, love and justice is *our* responsibility. While we are waiting on God to fulfil the promise, God is waiting on us to begin to live as if we believed the promise. So God is delaying because of God's patience with us. Indeed, God forbid that Jesus should come while we are so uninvolved with the world.

Secondly, God is slow, Peter writes, 'not wanting any to perish, but all to come to repentance' (v.9). God's reluctance has to do with God's compassion. It is not tardiness, or hardness of heart, but *mercy* we are witnessing here. The world, so beset with evil, under the spell of evil, is, and will remain, God's world. God will not give it up just like that. God hates the punishment the world invites, and seeks the repentance the world is so loath to come to, longs to show the mercy the world thinks it does not need.

With Sodom and Gomorrah, God first waits with punishment until God has 'gone down' to 'see' whether they have done according 'to the outcry' that has risen to heaven. God wants to 'know' before

God acts in judgement (Genesis 18:21). Wanting to 'know' means God is looking for excuses not to do what Sodom and Gomorrah deserve. For that reason God tarries with Abraham for that long, astonishing bargaining session, just in case some reason can be found for God to turn the divine wrath away.

While we tend to say, are *burning* to say, 'Come Lord Jesus, wipe the evildoers from the face of the earth!', God says, 'Is there another way?'. Even as we cry for the coming of the flood, God stays the waters at the sluice gates of heaven. While we relish the prospect of damnation and divine vengeance, God rejoices in the conversion of the sinner. This is so important a point that Ezekiel, whom we quoted just a while ago, finds it necessary to repeat it:

> As I live, says the LORD GOD, I have no pleasure in
> the death of the wicked, but that the wicked turn from
> their ways and live. Turn! Turn from your evil ways! Why
> would you die, O house of Israel? (33:11)

So the day of judgement is postponed, the wicked are given time to turn to God and be saved, even if one day has to be stretched into a thousand years.

My teacher at the Theological University at Kampen in the Netherlands, Gerard Rothuizen, said of this text: 'We know God as dove, as lamb, and as a lion. But even as a snail, He is impressive.'

IV

God is waiting on us to change, to learn to know the Lord, to do justice, to love mercy and to walk humbly with our God. God is waiting for us to understand that like God, we are not to condemn the world, but to love it. But what does God do, while waiting?

God is writing a book.

This is the remarkable response of the prophet Malachi to the doubters of his day who ask: 'Where is the God of justice?' (2:17), and, 'What do we profit by keeping God's commandments?' (3:14). For them, the world has not changed much. The arrogant are 'happy', and 'evildoers prosper'. They fear the LORD, and yet they speak these 'harsh words'. In verse 16 those who 'revere' the LORD spoke with one another, and 'the LORD took note and listened'.

Exegetes customarily say these are two different groups. Those who 'speak harsh words' cannot be the same as those who 'revered' the LORD. I beg to differ. For two reasons: First of all, those who are upset because of the prosperity of the evildoers and the undisturbed life of the arrogant are upset, not for themselves, but for the world. When evildoers prosper and the arrogant live unchecked in their power, there are always victims. And the victims are the poor, the weak and the powerless. So they are not concerned for themselves, but for those in the world who continue to suffer because the arrogant continue to prosper. It is therefore better to translate verse 14 thus: 'What gain is there in doing God's commandments?'. Their cry, 'Where is the God of justice?' is not a cry out of arrogance and cynical unbelief, but a cry of pain and distress. It is the same cry rent from the heart of the prophets and the Psalmist: 'How long, LORD?'. If it is rage, it is a holy rage, not against God, but against injustice. And where else can the believers go, but to God, with their pain, doubt, and anger? They are not saying, 'What good is it doing us?' They are saying, 'What good is it doing the world?'

But second of all, those who juxtapose these voices say true believers cannot rail against God like this. But they have forgotten Moses, Elijah, Jeremiah, and John the Baptist. Those angry voices are the same as the 'God-fearing' ones, the 'beloved' who believe that God listens when such angry questions are asked. God does not close God's ears and walk away in a huff when we pour out our anguished anger over the injustice in the world, over the pain of the weak, and the arrogance of the powerful. God listens. God 'takes note'.

But does God only listen? No, God writes a book – a 'book of remembrance'. Uh-oh, we think, God as bookkeeper, counting our sins on the debit side, our few good deeds on the credit side, until that great divine audit on Judgement Day. We might as well pack it in. It is a frightening thought. It is also an unworthy thought.

But it is no cash book God is keeping, it is a book of 'those who revered the LORD and thought on his name' (3:16). That means, only what we do for the LORD is written down. That is one of those heart-stopping thoughts from the Bible, so let me say it again. Only what we do for the LORD is written down. Sometimes we think what we do is futile; too little when measured against the powers that be and the challenges that face us. But before God, it is not forgotten. God remembers: every single deed of justice, every word of comfort, every protest against the wrong; every act of resistance to evil, however small. Every battle against racism or sexism; every 'no' against homophobia and exclusivism; every step in a march against women and child abuse, even when the numbers do not merit a news item. They will all be remembered. And what will be remembered by God is not whether we failed or succeeded, but that we tried, that we were faithful.

When the Day of the LORD comes, all this will be disclosed. It will be the day of God's judgement, yes, but it will also be the day of celebration of our righteousness. And those mishaps, all those missed opportunities? Forgotten, says Malachi. Those moments of despair and frustrated rage? Forgotten, says Malachi. And those times when I had not the courage, hope or love to set foot outside my door? When I was so swamped with self-pity that I could not bring myself to think of others? When I was so self-absorbed that the pain of others was way off my mind? Forgotten, says Malachi. Not written down.

V

God is waiting; for one deed of justice, one word of truth, one act of faith, one sign of revolt against evil. God waits. That is why Peter says, 'one day is as a thousand years ...'. God almost does not make it, the waiting becomes too much, and one day is like a thousand years. That is how we should read verse 8. God waits impatiently for us to do what is right, so that God can show mercy and compassion. Isaiah knew this too: 'The LORD longs impatiently to be gracious to you, and he rises to show you compassion' (30:18). Every day that God waits is like a thousand years.

But also, God feels our pain so acutely that every day that we suffer, every night that the poor go to bed hungry, every day justice is deferred for the powerless, is like a thousand years for God.

That one night in Nazi Germany, that would become history as 'Kristallnacht'; one night in Auschwitz; that one day in the torture chamber; one night of rape and pillage; one single day of war and 'ethnic cleansing'; that one day in Soweto when police for the first fired on children – it's like a thousand years! That one stretch in the hands of the South African Security police, the gory and unbelievable details which the general public only came to know partially through the Truth Commission – a thousand years! That pain that only a parent feels at the death of a child, or that moment when that child turns her back and walks out of your life – a thousand years!

And the opposite? That one thousand years are like one day? God does not only suffer with us, God also surprises us:

Four hundred and fifty years in Egypt – then suddenly: the exodus; Almost three hundred and fifty years of slavery, oppression and apartheid – and suddenly: liberation; Jesus is rejected, betrayed, accused, tried, dies on the cross – and suddenly it is Easter. That whole death lasts only three days.

It is for that reason that we must go on, for that reason we believe, for that reason that the church sings: We shall overcome.

We shall overcome, because God is patient, and loving and compassionate;

We shall overcome, because justice shall come down like waters, and righteousness like a mighty stream;

We shall overcome, because all things are possible for those who believe;

We shall overcome, because Jesus came, lived, died and rose from the dead;

We shall overcome because the Holy Spirit moves us, empowers us, burns within us;

We shall overcome, because God has promised, and we believe with Peter that in accordance with his promise, there will be a new heaven and a new earth where justice is at home, and where God's tent shall be pitched amongst God's people.

Deep in my heart, I do believe: we shall overcome.

The Iona Community is:

- An ecumenical movement of men and women from different walks of life and different traditions in the Christian church
- Committed to the gospel of Jesus Christ, and to following where that leads, even into the unknown
- Engaged together, and with people of goodwill across the world, in acting, reflecting and praying for justice, peace and the integrity of creation
- Convinced that the inclusive community we seek must be embodied in the community we practise

Together with our staff, we are responsible for:

- Our islands residential centres of Iona Abbey, the MacLeod Centre on Iona, and Camas Adventure Centre on the Ross of Mull

and in Glasgow:

- The administration of the Community
- Our work with young people
- Our publishing house, Wild Goose Publications
- Our association in the revitalising of worship with the Wild Goose Resource Group

The Iona Community was founded in Glasgow in 1938 by George MacLeod, minister, visionary and prophetic witness for peace, in the context of the poverty and despair of the Depression. Its original task of rebuilding the monastic ruins of Iona Abbey became a sign of hopeful rebuilding of community in Scotland and beyond. Today, we are about 250 Members, mostly in Britain, and 1500 Associate Members, with 1400 Friends world-wide. Together and apart, 'we follow the light we have, and pray for more light'.

For information on the Iona Community contact:
The Iona Community, Fourth Floor, Savoy House, 140 Sauchiehall Street, Glasgow G2 3DH, UK. Phone: 0141 332 6343
e-mail: admin@iona.org.uk   web: www.iona.org.uk

For enquiries about visiting Iona, please contact:
Iona Abbey, Isle of Iona, Argyll PA76 6SN, UK. Phone: 01681 700404
e-mail: ionacomm@iona.org.uk

Also from Wild Goose Publications ...

STATES OF BLISS AND YEARNING
The marks and means of authentic Christian spirituality
John L. Bell

Spirituality is not a permanent high, a continual blissed out state. To experience the heights, one has also to know the depths. In this book based on speeches and sermons delivered in marquees, cathedrals and local churches, John Bell deals with issues as diverse as private devotion and public debt. The picture of God that emerges is not one of a 'celestial sadist' but rather a compassionate being who asks that we do only what we can, starting from where we are, to be just and compassionate too.

John Bell is a minister of the Church of Scotland and a member of the Iona Community. He lectures and preaches throughout the English-speaking world. Along with his colleagues in the Wild Goose Worship and Resource Groups he has produced over fifty books and recordings containing congregational song and anthems, and dramatic, reflective and liturgical resources. He is also an occasional broadcaster on radio and television.

ISBN 978-1-901557-07-7

HARD WORDS FOR INTERESTING TIMES
Biblical texts in contemporary contexts
John L. Bell

In this second collection of sermons and addresses, John Bell proves that he is not one to shy away from the challenges provided by biblical stories. Likewise he proves startlingly adept at articulating the often uncomfortable questions the Bible poses for contemporary life. Paul, Job, Jeremiah, Elijah and Zachariah are among the biblical characters the author examines. His reflections cover a range of life issues and situations: from patience and love to transfiguration and death – and incisively, in the longest piece in the collection, the events of September 11th, 2001.

ISBN 978-1-901557-75-6

www.ionabooks.com

THE WAY AHEAD
Grown-up Christians
Ian M. Fraser

Ian Fraser has been a pastor-labourer in heavy industry, a parish minister, Warden of Scottish Churches House in Dunblane, an Executive Secretary of the World Council of Churches, and Dean and Head of the Department of Mission at Selly Oak Colleges, Birmingham. He is the author of nineteen books, including *Strange Fire*, *Salted with Fire* and the spiritual classic *Reinventing Theology*, which is used as a standard theological sourcebook around the world.

Ian is one of the original members of the Iona Community who helped George MacLeod to rebuild 'the common life' and the Abbey buildings on the isle of Iona. Throughout his life Ian has travelled the world, alone and with his wife, Margaret, visiting basic Christian communities. He has walked alongside slum dwellers in India and Haiti; Nicaraguan and Cuban revolutionaries; priests, nuns and catechists facing arrest and/or death in Central and South America; small farming and fishing communities in the Philippines … His life has been a search for the vision and reality of a church in which all voices are heard and all parts of Christ's body are included. One place where he found such a model was in the underground church in Eastern Europe during the Communist era. He writes about that discovery here, among other life experiences.

Eighty-eight years old now, Ian calls The Way Ahead his 'last will and testament', the capstone and distillation of his work and thinking. At a time when many people cannot see the future and feel that the church is dying, Ian feels hope and sees great possibility. He writes:

> It is difficult to read the signs of one's own time. In the West, are we at a time of a decline in Christian belief? I think that there is a chance that we are in Kingdom territory where humanity is shouldering church to the side – not rejecting it but giving it its true servant place – in favour of direct Kingdom priorities.

This is a book for anyone who cares about where the church is heading. Will the Christian church live or die? What is the way ahead?

Perhaps the church will live – if it has the courage and humility to take Ian Fraser's inclusive message to heart.

www.ionabooks.com

Wild Goose Publications, the publishing house of the Iona Community established in the Celtic Christian tradition of St Columba, produces books, tapes and CDs on:

- holistic spirituality
- social justice
- political and peace issues
- healing
- innovative approaches to worship
- song in worship, including the work of the Wild Goose Resource Group
- material for meditation and reflection

If you would like to find out more about our books,
tapes and CDs, contact us at:

Wild Goose Publications
4th Floor, Savoy House, 140 Sauchiehall Street, Glasgow G2 3DH, UK

Tel. +44 (0)141 332 6292
Fax +44 (0)141 332 1090
e-mail: admin@ionabooks.com

or visit our website at
www.ionabooks.com
for details of all our products and online sales